AWE
THE
AUTOMATIC
Writing
EXPERIENCE

AWE

THE

AUTOMATIC

Writing

EXPERIENCE

How to Turn Your Journaling into Channeling to Get
Unstuck, Find Direction, and Live Your Greatest Life!

MICHAEL SANDLER

MEDIA

Published 2021 by Gildan Media LLC
aka G&D Media
www.GandDmedia.com

Contact the author, Michael Sandler, at hello@inspirenationshow.com.
Find bonus materials and more on the automatic writing experience at www.AutomaticWriting.com.
Join Michael Sandler on his popular podcast: www.InspireNationShow.com and www.YouTube.com/InspireNationShow.

Book design by Diren Yardimli

Library of Congress Cataloging-in-Publication Data is available upon request

ISBN: 978-1-7225-0320-8

10 9 8 7 6 5 4 3 2 1

Contents

Praise for *AWE, The Automatic Writing Experience*

"Most of life's simple decisions are easy to make. Pizza or pasta? There's no great penalty for getting it wrong. But when it comes to the big ones, the stakes are high. Jim or Jeff? California or Costa Rica? Stocks or bonds? Wouldn't it be nice to consult a source of infinite wisdom when faced with a life-changing decision? That's exactly what Michael Sandler shows you how to do in *The Automatic Writing Experience*, using the apt acronym of AWE. He shows you how to set aside your worried, logical, limited mind, and connect with wellsprings of wisdom far below the level of conscious awareness. Science shows that the essence of the universe we live in is information, and Michael's AWE process puts you in touch with that awesome source. If you'd like to shift persistent or mysterious patterns of limitation in your life, you need to bypass your limited conscious habits. AWE is your step-by-step guide to tapping into the wisdom of the cosmos and the infinite potential available from that source."

—**Dawson Church**
Award-winning author of Bliss Brain: The Neuroscience of
Remodeling Your Brain for Resilience, Creativity and Joy

"*The Automatic Writing Experience* demonstrates why Michael Sandler is one of today's most dynamic, hands-on, and meaningful voices in practical spirituality. Michael demonstrates how the method of automatic writing brought him back from the brink—and how it can deliver breakthroughs in your life. This book is a user's manual to your inner resources."

—**MITCH HOROWITZ**
Author of *The Miracle Club*

"Automatic writing is a powerful spiritual practice that supports your personal connection to the divine. With his infectious, loving and enthusiastic energy, Michael Sandler will have you in alignment receiving powerful messages through this transformative experience. This book is an essential guide."

—**KYLE GRAY**
Best-selling author of *Angel Prayers and Raise Your Vibration*

"Drawing on an ancient practice and the latest in deep mind techniques, Michael Sandler helps you plug into the power Source that can guide you to manifest the life of your dreams. If you want to live an on-fire, AWE filled life, then this book is for you."

—**DR. JOE VITALE**
Author of *Zero Limits*

"Michael Sandler is an insightful and generous teacher, and many will find this book to be an invaluable tool for accessing the wisdom of the Higher Self."

—PAUL SELIG
Author of *Alchemy, A Channeled Text*

"Michael Sander's book, *The Automatic Writing Experience*, is a key tool for our life's toolbox. This fabulous book helps all of us to remain empowered, centered, and connected to Spirit.

Learning how to listen to your intuition and your direct spiritual guidance is the only way we move forward with our lives.

With his usual humor, compassion, love, inspiration and storytelling, Michael explains how automatic writing can be a powerful doorway for you during this time, blending the practical 'how to' with the magic of Spirit."

—SANDRA INGERMAN, MA
Award winning author of 12 books including
Walking in Light and *The Book of Ceremony*

"I totally agree with the benefits of *The Automatic Writing Experience*. I have been doing this for decades; keeping journals, writing poetry and books and more. Read what Michael has to share and help to know your true self and heal."

—BERNIE SIEGEL, MD
Author of *No Endings Only Beginnings* and with grandson Charlie Siegel, the
poetry book, *When You Realize How Perfect Everything Is*

❧

"Michael Sandler has bestowed upon us all a very precious and deeply healing gift with his new book. Most of us in the quiet time of writing feel inner peace and spiritual renewal. But until now only the inimitable Michael has pulled this perennial experience into a full-fledged spiritual practice to be engaged in with uplifting creative energies that arise from the very depths of our inner being. Every writer should pick up a copy right away. Fabulous job, Michael. We are cheering. Book of the year!"

—STEPHEN G. POST PHD
Founding director of the Institute for Research on
Unlimited Love and author of *Why Good Things Happen to Good People*

❧

"Michael Sandler's book on automatic writing will change your life, fundamentally. For the better!

Written in a no-nonsense and accessible style, and laced with his trademark mischievous yet grounding humour, Michael takes you through the process of automatic writing step-by-step in a way that is both easy to understand, and even easier to do.

He discusses how to access that inner wisdom that's available to everyone, if you know where to look and how to ask. As Michael points out, you don't need to be religious, spiritual or even believe in any kind of higher power—you just need to follow his simple technique and you'll find yourself connected to an infinite wisdom that's available to help guide you through life.

You don't need to know how to meditate. You don't need to go full lotus. You don't need to eat kale or chant mantras. You just need to follow Michael's method and you will find yourself communicating with a source of wisdom and love that knows what's best for you.

I found the book to be revelatory. It will change my life. I now have a simple and elegant technique that I can use to connect to my higher guidance. Woo Hoo!"

—BILL BENNETT
Author and Director of *PGS* and *Facing Fear*

❧

"A big 'Woo Hoo!' to Michael Sandler for taking the 'Woo Woo' out of automatic writing! He approaches what has long remained a mysterious process of attuning to higher guidance and makes it easy and accessible for all. Like everything Michael does, this wonderfully practical book is both entertaining and deeply spiritual at the same time. Put the insights you learn here to use, and your life may well be transformed."

—SUZANNE GIESEMANN
Author of *Messages of Hope* and *The Daily Way messages*

❧

"In *The Automatic Writing Experience* (AWE), Michael Sandler provides a proven process for illuminating the path of the most sacred journey we will every take—to self-love and self-worth. This book offers a potent compass anyone can follow, that you will return to again and again."

—NANCY LEVIN
Best selling author of *Setting Boundaries Will Set You Free*

❧

"Michael Sandler's AWE helps you come back to the perfect present moment, reclaim the power of your authentic self, and go beyond the egoic, worrying, thinking mind. It is an invitation to hear your inner spirit, and take your power back, so you can be, feel, think and do in your daily life. Michael's book will have you diving into AWE in no time, plugging into your inner spirit, and rediscovering your true power."

—ANNE BÉRUBÉ PH.D
Author of *Be Feel Think Do: A Memoir*

"Connecting to Spirit through automatic writing will enhance your life and the lives of everyone in your orbit.

Michael's expertise at receiving guidance from Spirit combined with his easy-to-follow approach will have you communicating with the heavens in record time."

—JULIE RYAN
Medical Intuitive, Medium and Psychic

"When you want to know more about something, you turn to a master. Michael Sandler is indeed one of those masters who, besides being one of my favorite thought teachers and coaches around, is offering a truly powerful tool, broken down step by step, that will transform how you use your mind. If you are someone who wants a personal transformation of how you think and communicate, but also has a desire to explore the untapped wisdom and spiritual guidance that is just waiting to come through you, this book is probably what you've been looking for."

—DR. MICHAEL LENNOX
Psychologist and Astrologer

"Michael Sandler's fascinating and illuminating book, *The Automatic Writing Experience* invites the reader to take a deep dive into discovering an inner oracle that we each possess–a deep knowing and inward directionality that comes about when we engage in spiritual practice and self-inquiry.

The wisdom in this book borrows from many different psychological, philosophical and spiritual traditions and merges them all into one unique system of Sandler's creation that offers us practical and simple practices that can bring us great healing and insight."

—**JONATHAN HAMMOND**
Author of *The Shaman's Mind—Huna Wisdom to Change Your Life*

"If you want to live your greatest life, way outside the box, and better than you ever imagined, then you need to dive into AWE. Michael Sandler's fascinating technique will help you separate from the pack, discover your authentic greatness, and find a completely new—and better way to live. If you want to live an awesome, awe-filled life, then dive into AWE with Michael."

—**BRANT PINVIDIC**
Author of *the 3 Minute Pitch,* CEO INvelop Entertainment

"You have an inner wisdom—that desperately wants to be heard! Michael's brilliant book gives you the tools to do it now. I love the title, the book and the profound answers he shares with each of us. Absorb and use the wisdom of an ability that he will help you master effortlessly. I am recommending everyone wanting to tap into their inner voice read it."

—**Mark Victor Hansen**
Co-author of the *Chicken Soup for the Soul* series and World's Bestselling Non-Fiction Author 500,000,000+ books sold

"Readers always ask me, 'Was that my sign? That billboard on I-70? That song on the radio from my childhood? Like me, they yearn for Spirit to communicate in neon. Using the writing process in this book, guidance becomes personal, custom-designed and reliable. Thanks, Michael, for this easy and benevolent communication device that outshines social media, Google and especially our own crippled, conditioned fear thoughts."

—**Pam Grout**
#1 New York Times bestselling author of 20 books including *E-Squared*, *Thank and Grow Rich*, *Art and Soul, Reloaded*, and *The Course in Miracles Experiment*

"Michael Sandler is my good friend. The universe connected us together. He understands the universe. He understands what you need in your self-help arsenal to manifest your dreams. And your arsenal should be simple—Pen. Paper. Dreams. That's it. This book shows you how to successfully manifest your desires and connect to the angels who are at our command. I am proof it works. This is serious life-saving stuff. *The Automatic Writing Experience* solidified my belief in the law of attraction, the angels, your higher self, and the laws of the universe. Listen to Michael, he knows what he's talking about. Study this book. Apply it. Reap your greatness!"

—**Michael Samuels**
Best-selling author of *Just Ask the Universe*

Special Message
from Dr. Ervin Laszlo

M ichael is on to something here—to something that is
entirely true and entirely fundamental. We can contact
and communicate with the world—this means we can
connect—or reconnect—to what I have been calling
"the source." We have known this—all serious, insightful people have
known it. But one of the important tools for connecting was missing
from our set of instruments: the AWE.

I now ask myself, did I have the AWE—automatic writing experience? Did I actually do automatic writing? At first sight, this sounds
unlikely. I and nobody and nothing else wrote what I wrote. But on
second thought, I am not so sure. Not so sure that I ALONE have written what I have written. Let me tell you my experience.

I have not written anything by hand for the past thirty years at
least—too slow for me . . . I used to be a concert pianist so my fingers
are nimble, and I type fast on a keyboard. Almost, but not quite as,
fast as I can think. Now the computer saves it for me. I first write
the way it comes, and then I read and reread, and revise and revise

until I am satisfied. But what emerges first is not something I worked out beforehand. I know the context and the issue of course, and I focus on it. But then I let go and write. Doing this is like a physical urge. If I can't put my hand on a keyboard right away, I almost feel sick—I can't think of anything else, and certainly can't do most anything else—relaxation and sleep are out of the question. When I do sit down and write, the sentences form by themselves—I just have to write them down. Is this automatic writing? Is it channeling? Is it a form of inspiration? Is it communing with a superhuman or at least nonhuman intelligence?

To me, this experience is a deep source of awe and wonder. I am not alone in writing what I do—I have help. A dictation of sorts, but by no means a random one. It is highly focused on the questions I address. But it flows. And—I should add, it can also block. It doesn't always flow, and the way it's blocked is sometimes quite amazing. E-mail fails to go through, paragraphs I have written disappear from the file, and on occasion an entire file becomes inaccessible. Where it goes, I don't know. But why it goes, I can guess. Because on thinking again on what I have written—or tried to write—I realize that it's off the mark. I have taken a wrong turn—introduced a wrong hypothesis, or misphrased something I wanted to convey. In retrospect I can say, thank goodness it disappeared!

Then there is the positive case. When I reread and consider what I have written and it checks with what I see as the relevant evidence—other people's experiences, or a theory or affirmation coming from science—then I am amazed and elated.

So good to know that I am not at the mercy of my own devices when I expose an idea or a theory—that there is "something"—or someone?—who works with me. Supervises me and prevents me from making at least major blunders.

Thank you, dear Michael, for prompting me to think about this experience. I have never written it down, although I share it with my wife quite often—every time I am amazed and either dismayed or elated. Now I can get further feedback from you and your readers—from people who share a keen and hopefully unbiased interest in the phenomenon of AWE. And feel the awe it inspires themselves.

DR. ERVIN LASZLO, Two-time *Nobel Peace Prize Nominee* and Winner of the *Goi Peace Prize, the International Mandir of Peace Prize,* the *Conacreis Holistic Culture Prize,* and *The Polyhistor Prize of the Environmental Protection.*

Foreword

Hello happy readers! Want to enjoy more peace of mind? Read—and do—this book!

I first met Michael in January of 2020 as an invited guest on his podcast, *Inspire Nation*, when we were discussing my new book, *The Healthy Brain Book*. Even virtually Michael radiated vibes, some inner force from his mind into my mind that brought me peace just by watching and listening to his body language. His podcast jumped to the top of my must-see list.

In AWE Michael and Jessica reflect similar vibes as they do in their podcast. You, the reader, will feel a cerebral connection with these two trusted authors as the words from their hearts and minds leave you feeling: "This is just what I need. This is just how I want to feel."

Their term "AWE" (Automatic Writing Experience) belongs in the mental wellness toolbox of every reader who is inspired to take charge of their brain health. I was literally "in awe" at the end of reading sections that left me feeling, "That makes sense!"

AWE takes you inside your brain while writing. You will be in awe to learn how putting your pen to paper relaxes your brain better than do fingers to keyboard. When you're in the mood to write, your brain particularly loves poetry. One day while writing on the beach this poem naturally overtook my mind:

The loveliness of the land
The softness of the sand
The serenity of the sea
God gave this to me

I remember my favorite spiritual director, Mom, giving me her advice for boredom and upsetting behavior: "Go outside and play!" AWE inspires: "Go outside and write."

Creative writing also inspires deeper connections with your loved ones by helping you write what you feel. One day as I was writing, Martha walked by and another poem naturally came to me:

I feel that I shall never see
A lady as lovely as you are to me.

AWE is the anecdote to ANTs was my top take-home point while reading this book. ANTs (automatic negative thoughts) clutter the minds of so many persons now living in a world of fake news and fear factors. At no time in history has the need for mental wellness tools been so necessary, and why this book is so timely.

Michael's story about his ADHD reminds me of when Martha and I were on "Good Morning America" discussing our ADD book. Joan Lunden asked Martha, "Where did you get the material for your book?" Martha promptly replied, "It's my husband's autobiography!"

As you will read in Michael's testimony, ADD *is* a *difference,* not a *disorder.* Some very highly-creative and highly-sensitive brains are wired differently. We don't try to "change" these unique brains. Instead, we "channel" them into the path God created them to have. AWE helps you stay on the path toward your personal peace recipe.

Every day in my medical practice, I advise troubled junior and senior minds: "Find your happy path and carry your personal toolbox to stay on it."

Of course, all minds are unique, so all mental wellness tools in this book may not fit the spiritual path of everyone. Yet, without worry or judgment, take the tools that keep you on your personal spiritual path.

Readers, you will be in awe about the section on meditation and the attitude-of-gratitude. No matter how life sucks, and in these troubled times it does, we all have a few things to be thankful for. I begin most mornings with what I call my "movement meditation." I move my body (walking or swimming) in rhythm with my mantra, such as:

Thank you God for my life (80 years).
Thank you God for my wife (54 years).
Thank you God for my health (cancer survivor).
Thank you God for my wealth (eight kids).
Thank you God for my MD.
Please make it my ministry.

AWE, my mind is in awe. Thank you, sincere Sandlers, for giving readers and followers a toolbox for happier and healthier living.

WILLIAM SEARS, MD, coauthor of *The Healthy Brain Book: An All Ages Guide to a Calmer, Happier, Sharper You.*

Introduction

Before I started practicing AWE (the automatic writing experience), I was lost, confused, literally in pain, and wiped out, financially and emotionally. Fortunately, I turned to AWE and heard I was to start a podcast (the *Inspire Nation* show) and to interview the best experts from around the world.

Now my wife, Jessica, and I are living our dreams with our miracle rescue animals including a rooster, yes, a rooster, and our show is one of the top spiritual self-help shows in the world, with millions of views and listens.

It all came out of automatic writing. All of the goodness, all of the magic, all of the miracles. And the same can happen for you.

What you hold in your hands now, or electronically on the screen before you, is a true miracle. It's a system that anyone can follow that will allow you to tap into your inner wisdom or the Divine.

Not sure where to turn? AWE can help. Health on the rocks? AWE can help. Freaked out by a pandemic, civil unrest, or the latest nightmare? AWE can help too. And certainly if you're struggling to mani-fest, to get back on your feet, or want to take your wealth and finances to a new level, then AWE is for you. For AWE is a rocket ship when it comes to manifestation.

And if you're struggling, stressed out, worried, anxious, depressed, or worse, then AWE will give you not just solace, but can help heal your mind, help transform the swirling energies inside and outside of you, rewire your subconscious, and help you transform your wounds into powerful, positive energy—for positive change even greater than you could ever imagine.

Automatic writing is a tool that's been used in psychology to rewire the subconscious by the likes of Jung and Freud, for well over 150 years. The technique may have become a bit lost to modern psy-chologists, but it's on its way back—more on this in the history section.

In December 2019, I interviewed a brilliant astrologer, Dr. Michael Lennox. And together, well before COVID-19, we called 2020 the Year of Reckoning, meaning everything that we've swept under the carpet, or didn't want to deal with, would have to be faced. Boy, was that true!

But now, I call this time period moving forward the Era of Rein-vention. It is a time of tremendous possibilities. Yes, there's swirling energy all around us. Yes, it seems like Armageddon or worse. But nothing could be further from the truth.

When you learn how to plug in, to connect with the Universe, con-nect with your wisdom, or connect with your guides, you'll learn how special this time is, why your soul chose to incarnate during this time, how special you are, and what you are capable of doing—and where to go from here.

This time period is a springboard for powerful, positive possibili-ties. Not gloom and doom. Not even close, but a time of complete and total reinvention, where almost anything you dream of is possible.

Mind is creator. This is the basic tenet of the entire New Thought movement. Or as you've heard from the likes of Bob Proctor and Rhonda Byrne from *The Secret*, what we think about, we bring about—what they call the law of attraction.

Whatever we think about, focus on, and speak or write about, we can literally draw into existence. Of course, this means be careful what you wish for. But it also means you are the most incredible creator in the world. You just need to learn how to harness that energy, and in your hands is the tool. AWE can show you how to change your life, how to up-level everything, how to move past wounds and emotional blocks, and how to call yourself toward the most incredible, outrageous, over-the-top magnificent future that's so far beyond your wildest dreams—but is already waiting for you.

In this book—truly a manual for connecting with the Divine for guidance, manifestation, healing, and especially rewiring your subconscious, or for the atheists out there, for connecting with your inner wisdom—you will be guided step by step on how to tap in, get guidance, and discover the magical world that's already present in the here and now.

While I'm an angels guy and an alchemist, you don't have to believe in anything to get magic out of this book. But follow the directions, and you will blow yourself away.

For whether we call them angels, guides, light workers, or simply your inner wisdom, or even the quantum field of intelligent energy, there is a deep and profound wisdom just waiting to guide you, if only you would ask.

As the energies are swirling all around us, as COVID-19 leaves its mark, I have just one question to ask: If not now, then when? If you're not willing to make great change now, if you're not willing to dive into your soul, if you're not willing to take the leap of faith and seek out a different way—if not now, then when?

For this tool called AWE is pure magic, it will connect you with the other side. It will help you find your purpose, your path, your unique direction, and answer life's deepest questions for you, like why did I incarnate during this time? Why did I choose this life? Why did I choose these struggles? And how in the world can I turn all of this around me into the greatest positive? How can I transform my life so that I am truly rocking it, on purpose, on path, and doing exactly what I'm supposed to do?

And how can I feel happy—especially now? Let's see.

1 | Welcome to the AWE-Inspiring World of Automatic Writing

I awaken quietly at 4:30 a.m. The world is silent, even the hummingbirds haven't risen yet. I run through some gratitudes in my head, as Jessica sleeps silently beside me. From there, I move stealthily down the stairs, to the bathroom, grab a cup of hot water and minerals, take my vitamins, then it's on to the studio.

Within my studio sanctuary I go silent, meditate, and then put on my headphones and some peaceful theta brain-entrainment music. The sound of birds chirping at the beach can be heard between my ears.

I go to my Google drive, open a new automatic writing document (I used to use pen and paper, but the words come so fast I can't keep up) and lean back in my chair. It's still nearly pitch-black outside, with just a tiny hint of purple above the horizon.

As my eyes slink closed, I write out my first prayer, then another, welcoming in assistance, angels and guides, and especially loved ones who've crossed over to the other side.

As my prayers finish, the words begin to flow. My fingers take on a life of their own, as profound wisdom spills out onto the page. I know it's not from me, as I'm still half asleep. But paragraph after paragraph spill out, one faster than the next. Occasionally I'll interject and ask a question, but most often, I simply bear witness to the guidance coming from beyond.

Hello, bright and shiny beacons of light! This description of my process for automatic writing reflects its simple ritual and beauty. Please allow me to show you how to tap into your inner wisdom and discover your greatest guidance through this ancient art.

Imagine being able to talk to a higher power, whatever you wish to call this force or belief. To communicate your every wish, thought, query, and desire and to hear an answer, clear as day.

How would this change your life?

When you sit down and initiate your ritual for automatic writing, and put pen to paper, this is exactly what happens. Whether you believe in a god, source, Universe, or simply your guiding inner wisdom, you briefly meditate, go into prayer, and then your pen begins to write—almost without thought.

Sound too good to be true?

One of my coaching clients, Mary H., told me, "Automatic writing has been a real life-changing experience for me that has become a part of my daily routine most days. The process set me free from unforgiveness that I didn't realize I had toward my late mom and myself. Through writing and my coaching, the groundedness and opening up of the flood gates of my heart has happened through automatic writing, showing me areas of my life to align with this legacy I want to leave here on earth, a legacy of love."

From David: "Automatic writing helps me enjoy the journey, adding a spice of excitement to my morning to start my day. It has awakened my heart. I don't think I know any of us who doesn't have a relationship where we don't necessarily hold somebody in a beautiful light. We can find peace and solace in automatic writing either by literally, quite literally writing to [those who have passed on] and connecting to their essence, connecting to their soul or connecting to that inner wisdom part of us that can speak for them."

On a more practical daily level, Nicole, a banker, said, "I was having a disagreement with my boss—so many knives in my back at work. I asked myself what I could do about this. Automatic writing helped me in the most fantastical way."

Through automatic writing, Nicole was able to see what was going on from other people's perspectives. Then she actually started getting confirmation from her bosses as to why these events were taking place. Automatic writing shared with her a road map of how she could either heal the relationship or become such a superwoman in the process that that experience and the knives in her back actually became positive fuel to make her a better human being.

Loosely speaking, automatic writing has been the process used by authors and sages for thousands of years. Have you ever known someone who said, "A book just came to me"? Their fingers flew as they wrote or typed as if the Universe was sending them a message, and they were the vehicle to deliver the message.

The Universe will answer if you ask.

Many years ago, Jessica and I were nearly bankrupt. Meanwhile, I was making a comeback from a near-fatal accident, and she was ill with mold toxicity. Our lives were crumbling, despite the fact we were living in paradise on Maui. With so many challenges, we were overwhelmed.

But once I put pen to paper with automatic writing, that all began to change. With one simple question, "What do I need to know today?" the puzzle pieces began to come together and our lives began to change quite dramatically.

We learned we had to start a show, the *Inspire Nation* show to be exact, now one of the top self-help and spirituality podcasts worldwide and wildly popular YouTube channel. We learned I had to get my life coaching going again, something I'd been doing for almost twenty years. I now coach and teach hundreds to thousands of people each week, one-on-one or through Zoom meetings.

And we learned each step of what we needed to do to help Jessica heal, recover our finances, get back on track with life, and live a miraculous life—wherever we are—whether we're in a dream home high above a Rocky Mountain town, nestled in the foothills, with trails and animals all around or traveling the US in a massive RV and experiencing the magic and majesty of our national parks.

As it was with Mary, Julio, and Nicole and so many others whose lives have been touched and transformed by automatic writing (and you'll hear more of the stories shared by AWE practitioners in the chapters ahead), so much of our success has come out of automatic writing.

Quieting the Monkey-Mind

Our minds are going a million miles an hour, telling us to turn right, turn left, go here, don't go there, or even telling us to freeze in our tracks. There's no winning with our minds, as the voices can be overwhelming, fear-based, and contradictory at best.

Worse still, the voices in our heads aren't even ours. They're the voices of the collective, the tribe, our parents, the news, our egos, or who knows what, but they're not the voice of wisdom—and certainly not voices coming from our hearts.

But when you go into automatic writing, you quiet the incessant chatter of the monkey mind, and you turn up your intuition. You're able to plug back into a knowing that's always been there. To a loving, kind, and gentle voice that can give you a big-picture perspective of your life, where to go, where not to, and the safest, easiest way to get there.

With the automatic writing experience—I call it AWE—confusion starts to melt away. You feel more at peace, more in alignment, and in greater accord with the world around you. In essence, you find your flow.

What you hold in your hands in the AWE-inspiring process is pure magic. A technique once available only to the prophets and sages, through the automatic writing experience, you have the ability to tap into the voice of the god you follow, the voice of the angels, or the voice of your highest guides, and you can get guidance on every aspect of your life.

Want to know your path in life? AWE has the answers.

Want to know why you're struggling? AWE knows that too.

Want to know how to manifest, attract abundance, or attract the life of your dreams. It's in AWE.

AWE gives you direct access to a higher intelligence, a voice inside or outside of you that never lies, will never steer you wrong, and will help you lead your greatest, most authentic, heart-centered, joyous life—with far fewer struggles and less strife—if only you would listen.

It's the voice that's always been inside of you, that small, still voice that will never steer you wrong. Just listen.

The power is inside of each and every one of us. When you've heard "don't go down that dark alley," that's the voice of AWE. And when you've yanked the steering wheel to the side away from danger, almost before knowing why, the voice that yelled "turn now" to avoid an oncoming truck is AWE as well.

It's like having your own internal GPS, the ability to tune in and get direction, in a moment's notice.

How AWE Works

Angels are my thing, so, to me, that intuition is our guardian angels at work. But whether you call it angels, guides, higher self, God, or simply your inner wisdom, that voice is always there, always loving, and always waiting to give you a guiding hand. We only need to reach out and take it.

So how does the automatic writing experience called AWE work?

In simplest terms, early on, you'll learn powerful, but incredibly easy meditation techniques for even the most ardent non-meditator (you don't need to learn how to become a monk or sit in a cave) to quiet the mind and stop the incessant chatter. For when we have a dozen competing stations playing in our mind, it's hard to hear anything, let alone a voice of wisdom, so this process will help you dial back those voices and learn to crank up your greatest inner voice.

After learning basic meditations in this book, you'll learn some key simple prayers to step you down into a deeper trance-like state. From a neuroscience perspective, you'll be entering a theta brain wave state where your thinking mind goes quiet and your expansive spiritual mind opens.

And from there, you'll learn a basic process, or ritual, that helps you step down even further into the wisdom and words that have always been there waiting for you. Of course, you'll learn advanced techniques as well—for guidance, for manifestation, even for talking with deceased loved ones and Mother Earth.

There's no limit to where you can go with AWE.

Why do I call it AWE? Because *awe* is the last thing you feel when you feel spun, all alone, and directionless—like a piece of wood floating out in a vast ocean. But when you can hear the voice of angels, or the voice of God, your jaw drops, your heart expands, and you know, once and for all, you're not alone, never were alone, and never will be alone again. That sense of awe and wonder that fills your heart gives you greater courage, strength, and guidance to live life again, and at a completely different level.

In essence, AWE is the state you get into through automatic writing where your pen is moving at a flurry and the words continue to flow. And they're not coming from you. You get direction, clarity, almost a postmortem on everything that's gone "wrong," but most importantly you get a higher-level perspective on life and a vehicle where you can ask the Divine or your inner wisdom any question you want. And you get reassurance that you're not alone, that you'll get through this, and that everything is all right, perfect in its own divine way, and can get even better.

Unlike prayer, with AWE you ask questions and actually get answers. If you simply turn the page, you'll learn how to access this inner wisdom in a matter of just days or weeks. And it's not magic, and not simply accessible to the few. Automatic writing doesn't require a special gift, a highly trained sense of intuition, or years in a cave honing your skills. It just takes a desire to plug in, to hear from the Divine, and a little bit of practice to get the words flowing. But there's no one who can't plug in, no one who can't get steering from the Divine.

Why? Because each one of us has heard this voice, or had a gut feeling or intuitive hit. We've each yanked the wheel at the last second to avoid an accident, or known who was calling before we even picked up the phone.

It's this inner wisdom we're tapping into, that's always been there, just waiting for us to ask.

What Automatic Writing Is Not

What if you go into automatic writing and say, "I need five ideas to sell millions of books next year?" That level of expectation, at least early on, crushes you in AWE. What do you mean? Can't AWE help with anything? Absolutely.

But when you say, "I need," you've now gone to your head, to ego, and you're demanding that the bus driver tell the mapmaker where to go. It doesn't work that way. Instead, we get to go through this AWE process and say, "Hey, I'm interested in having some best sellers next year. What can you tell me? Where can you guide me? Is that reasonable? How do we get there?"

Rather than saying (almost like putting a gun to AWE's head), "You will give me my best sellers or a million dollars right now," and AWE would go, "Eek." Imagine what it would be like going into online dating and saying, "You will sleep with me on the first date." And the connection is thinking, "I don't even know your name yet." Of course, AWE knows more about you than you do, but it's a process whereby you get to develop a relationship with AWE. Until that relationship's developed, it's hard to get the deepest wisdom and just too easy to think you're in AWE when you're really in your head (more about ego in a later chapter).

We have to allow things to progress at whatever pace they are meant to. If we stick with AWE as a daily practice, it's amazing how fast you'll start to get deeper wisdom.

Automatic Writing Is Not Journaling

Journaling is a first-person writing experience. It's all about the first-person *I, me, my*. Whereas, automatic writing is a second-person writing experience. It's about you. You are loved. You are good. You get to be more patient. And you are all right.

Journaling is coming from the egoic thinking mind. We're just writing about what's taken place, what we're worried about, and analytical answers to our problems. As Einstein said, you can't solve a problem from the level of energy from which it was created. That's what journaling is. It's coming from your thinking mind.

Contrast this with AWE, which is coming from a higher wisdom, whether you call it inside or outside of yourself, below or above. But it's outside of your day-to-day thinking, and so it'll have higher-level, far better answers.

Don't get me wrong, journaling is a helpful practice. Journaling helps you get ideas out on paper that you may not have thought of and does help you to step back and look at your life and say, "What's going on here?" And it can be quite the cathartic process.

But journaling doesn't help you step the aperture far enough back that you really separate it from the experience. When you dive into AWE, you can step back from yourself—in spiritual terms, you become the infinite observer or the one who cheers you on in life, rather than participates in it. When you step back and get this infinite observer perspective, everything changes, especially the guidance you get. For you're no longer stuck in the trenches but observing from far above. It is a completely different process from journaling.

Automatic writing comes from that inner wisdom, angels, guides, Universe, Source, or as I like to joke, the giant cheeseburger in the sky—whoever and whatever you want to call it. It's the voice on the inside that says, "It's okay, Michael. It's all right for you to look at your world and the totality of it. Let me show you some things that you may not have noticed by being stuck in the role of the I."

AWE Is Not Your Crystal Ball

While I write in AWE daily, if not multiple times a day, and can hear that voice now loud and clear throughout the day, and especially when coaching, I do not rely on it to tell me what's going to happen in the future.

First, it'll rarely tell me because the future hasn't been written, not by anyone. Okay, there are an infinite number of multiverses, and they're all taking place at once, but that's beyond the scope of this book. For our purposes, we live in a free-will universe, so who knows what will happen?

That's why when I coach or teach I say, "My crystal ball is broken"—for there are just too many elements going on to know what's coming when. Of course, AWE would say that'd take away the surprise, and where's the fun in that?

More importantly, when we try to predict the future, we often get out of that heart-centered, AWE-some place and right back into head. We start thinking, conjecturing, and scheming about what the future may look like, and that's not AWE.

When I ask in AWE what's coming next, I hear one thing consistently, time after time: "You're not supposed to know the answers right now." In essence, this time of extreme uncertainty is here to help us grow, to help us dive into our spiritual nature, to help us let go of the outcome, and to help us heal the deepest darkest wounds, which are coming out now more than ever. If we had the answers, then we wouldn't be able to expand, grow, or heal. In essence, when things are spoon-fed to us, why do we need to learn anything?

AWE is also not great for big, life-changing decisions in the beginning. Over time you can use AWE for anything you can think of. But initially, with big, heavy, scary decisions, your egoic mind is likely to kick back in. For instance, if your concern is about finances, big moves, or even whether to stay married or not—great questions to ask about in AWE—initially take the answers with a major grain of salt. Rather than looking at specific answers, look for themes or patterns over time.

Automatic Writing Is Not Your Ouija Board

While some might consider using the Ouija board as a form of automatic writing, this is not the method I am presenting in this book. So not to worry, I'm not taking you on an out-of-body experience or having your hand get taken over by a spirit. You'll retain control of your hand and your entire body for that matter. You are not getting possessed by another entity in any way, shape, or form. *You* are physically writing, not someone or something else.

The messages are channeled through your mind first. Once your brain registers, it sends signals to your hand to write out the message. If you were a natural-born or practiced medium, you wouldn't need the writing part at all. But for most of us who were not born with the natural ability to channel or spent a great amount of time practicing this skill, the act of writing helps our brains tune into the messages.

Automatic Writing Is Not Dictation

Again, while some might consider dictation a form of automatic writing, this is not what I'm teaching. I'm not teaching you how to channel a booming voice in your head. The only voice you'll likely hear in your head is your own. It's your own internal voice that is relaying the messages coming through.

* * *

This section has looked at what AWE is not. But here is a lovely spot to tell you, in the words of one of my students, what AWE is—because I could not say this better than Miguel has:

> A pencil, a rubber band, the chair on which you sit becomes a profound unintended metaphor to explain life, consciousness and the greatness of it all. This sense of awe is visceral as you wonder at the grace and beauty and magnitude of our interconnected Universe. And you feel so whole and so complete and so with everything. There is nothing to need or want or do, except write another heart-stopping word. Beyond the mere cognitive, beyond the material. It erupts through you. A volcano from somewhere unseen. You are mesmerized with emotion.
>
> By life itself . . .
> By the infinite . . .
> By Spirit . . .
>
> And the words just pour forward from your being with no need to delete. No wants, no regrets or edits. Isn't that a life in resonance with a spiritual master? Surely life is for these moments. These moments of AWE.

Three What-if Questions about AWE

1 | What if I can't write, I'm not a writer?

I love it when people say they can't write, or they hate to write. Why? Because they're often the first ones into AWE and end up with the most profound words of wisdom—and it's so easy to tell it's not coming from them.

So if you think you can't write, then perfect. It means your thinking mind won't be involved because you're not doing the writing.

It's something I discussed with Andrew Newberg, MD. He's a neuroscientist who found that when people get into automatic writing, the part of the brain that normally writes—the frontal lobe responsible for your executive functions including writing—powers down or reduces blood flow. So for those in AWE, the part of the brain responsible for writing goes offline.

Why is this important? Because if you've trained for years and years to build up your writing skills, you're in essence strengthening your frontal lobe, and now we need it to go offline. But if you've never strengthened it for writing, it's actually easier to power down.

And once you power down, then you open up to a whole new world. That's when consciousness, or your inner wisdom, or your angels come out to play. For when you get out of your writing mind, you more quickly get into AWE.

You don't have to write for a long time, or think you'll fatigue or get writer's cramp, or that you'll be stuck writing for hour after hour—or having flashbacks of bluebooks and essays or exams (remember those days?). For you'll simply sit back, allow the pen to flow, and when it's done, it's done—or you could even set a timer to make sure you finish in ten or twenty minutes. This is not about efforting, it's about letting go at worst, or playing at best. But there's nothing you need to write, no word count, no page count, nothing. In fact if you just write gibberish for ten minutes, that's fine too.

Again, your aversion to writing and fear about writing actually will make your automatic writing more effective. The fact that writing is not your natural game—as Austin Powers said, "It's not my bag, baby"—is going to help you to write even better than somebody who skillfully crafts words with their mind, because their mind has an easier time of getting in the way.

If writing truly is not your bag (more specifically if you have some sort of condition such as severe arthritis that prevents you from actually holding a pen or typing), I've known people who dictate, you could call it "automatic speaking," and the most amazing words flow through them. However, unless you truly have some sort of condition, I would hold off and practice, practice, and practice first. Why? Because in automatic speaking, it's even easier to get tripped up by the thinking words of your mind. Therefore, if you're going to do automatic speaking, you'll want to record on your computer or a recording device on your phone or even an mp3 player to capture your words and, even better still, try speech-to-text software to help convert the spoken word to text.

2 | What if I'm afraid of letting negative spirits in?

I call this one the Ouija board question. It seems in Ouija, you never know which spirit you're going to call in. But with the AWE process, your intention prayer will serve a special purpose.

In essence, your intention prayer, which I will explain soon, is surrounding you in a protective bubble of love and light, and you're calling in only the highest energy or highest level spirits. In all of my experience, this has worked nearly 100 percent of the time.

A word of caution: While I'm not concerned about you channeling uninvited spirits (as long as you follow the process I outline in the next few chapters, that is, use your prayers), there are rare situations in which someone may not be well suited for the AWE process.

I have a dear friend who once did pranayama breathing (which is alternate nostril breathing), and his bipolar tendencies threw him into a manic episode. So while I have never seen that happen with AWE, I'm going to put in my fine print here. If you have manic tendencies, or substantial bipolar challenges, or are prone to schizophrenia or multiple-personality disorders, I would not attempt AWE. It'd be too difficult to determine who is saying what. Once any complex mental health issues are under control and your psychiatrist gives you the okay, that's a different story, but for now, I'd hold off.

3 | What if I don't have time?

This is a favorite question, because I like to flip it on its head. There's a zen koan that says, if you don't have time to meditate, meditate twice as long. And to riff off that paradox, I'd say, if you don't have time to do AWE, do AWE twice as long. Why? Because AWE will help you find more time in the day, find your blind spots, become more efficient, and quite literally give you more time. It's why, even when I'm at my busiest or my clients are at their busiest, I have them do AWE. For it sets them up for success for the day and gives them time back.

Now certainly if you have to take care of the kids or farm animals and you can't get up in time, then we need to look at how to rearrange your schedule, but, absolutely, you still get to do AWE. No matter how challenging it seems in the beginning, you will thank yourself for it.

The Process

In this book, I take you on a step-by-step approach, just as I do in my online training and boot camps. Everything you need to know about the automatic writing process is in this book. I hope to answer your questions about the practice as we move ahead. I simply ask that you follow the technique as closely as you can BEFORE you make changes to it.

Automatic writing is more than just a process of writing out ideas. It's a dynamic, time-tested, and systematic experience for gaining direct access to your higher self. When you have a process for accessing the wisdom of your higher self on a daily basis, you will become what I call a bright and shiny beacon of light. You'll be able to use automatic writing to tap into your intuition and begin getting wisdom and guidance today.

In the pages ahead, you will learn the best environment for the practice, what to say before you begin, how to begin, and the best questions to ask for daily guidance and direction. You'll troubleshoot your daily challenges and receive answers that pertain specifically to what works best for you. You'll purge negativity and start healing your inner wounds. You'll get on the path of discovering who you really are, why you are here, and what you are meant to do.

Shall we begin?

2 | Create the Optimal Environment for Your Automatic Writing Experience

S etting the stage for your automatic writing experience (AWE) is as much a part of the process as the actual writing.

Each year I train thousands of people in automatic writing. They want to know when they should tap into the Universe for answers. Early morning? Late night? They ask where AWE should be practiced—outdoors? In bed? A comfy chair? In yoga posture on the floor?

And they want to know the initial steps to step down into the trance-like state of AWE.

Every person eventually evolves their own technique, but I start here, in this chapter, with the basics that answer the questions about where, when, and some beginning steps for you to create your own automatic writing experience.

AWE Is in the Ritual

I like to say that everything in life is ritual, or can be ritual. What does this mean? It means that we can live life consciously, as if everything were sacred and everything were ceremony.

Not only does this enrich our lives, but it gives even more opportunities to connect with the Divine, spirits, or our inner wisdom, whether driving down the road, at the office, working out, in prayer, or especially in AWE. For everything is and can be made sacred.

Now what's the difference between ritual and ceremony? Ceremony is the activity, ritual is how you get there. So your wedding is a ceremony, but the ritual is the act, walking down the aisle, what's said, the ring slipped on the finger, the kiss.

When I used to hold space at a meditation center, my practice was filled with ritual. There was the lighting of the candles and the incense and even the ringing of the bell. The importance of ritual is this: it primes you for a change in brain wave state.

Ritual is an important method for getting yourself in a particular brain wave state or in the zone. In my discussion with neuroscientist Andrew Newberg, MD, we called it priming the brain.

Baseball players do it by swinging the bat and maybe even going into prayer before they step up to bat. Tennis players bounce the ball several times before they toss it in the air before serving up an ace. Golfers do it with a practice swing. Guitar players do it by tuning their guitar. We all have ways we use ritual to shift our focus and take us from an ordinary mindset to one highly focused for the event ahead.

With AWE, the more we go into ritual, the easier it is for us to connect. From the minute you wake up, you're stepping yourself down into AWE. As silly as it sounds from emptying the bladder, getting a drink, going into meditation, putting on the music, and going into your prayers, which I introduce in the next chapter, each event steps you further and further down the rabbit hole until, voila, you are in a state of AWE.

That's one of the key reasons, even after all these years, I don't skip a step when going into AWE. For I find the results far more profound when I go down the entire ladder, rather than trying to skip the rungs.

With that said, it's time to dive into the AWE process, which we can now also refer to as the AWE ritual, beginning with when to start your ritual.

The Importance of Early Mornings

I hear the groans from the I'm-not-a-morning-person readers. If you're not a bright and shiny beacon of light first thing in the morning, that's fine. However, to improve your chances of success and plug into your deepest guidance, it's highly recommended you do your automatic writing first thing in the morning (unless a different time of the day works better for you).

While there are no rules, when the whole world is asleep, it's much easier to hear the voice of AWE. Once you've secured the connection, then experiment with other times of day.

So please allow me to explain the AWE ritual when I do it and when most people prefer: in early morning. Once you understand why I have suggested early morning and you've given it your best try, you can decide what is best for you.

Ideally you'd get up before the rest of the world around you gets up. But to start, what if you were to get up just fifteen minutes before you normally do? You want to go to the bathroom and get yourself some water if you wish. I strongly recommend against anything caffeinated, at least until after your AWE practice. A hot herbal tea might nicely warm you on a chilly winter morning. You want to remain in a half-awake, sleepy state.

The Best Places to Write

Find your way to your sacred space. What does your favorite place look like? It could be a chair by your bed or a separate room in the house or apartment. Perhaps a room on a different floor where you can be alone.

I've worked with coaching clients who use the bathroom as a sacred place because they can gain some temporary privacy from the rest of the family including dogs, cats, and kids. I've even talked with people who have a quiet space in a closet, a nook under the stairs, a corner. You might prop the pillows and sit on your bed or even sit on a cushion next to your bed.

Whatever it may be, find a dark place where you can close the curtains, block the rising sun and any outside light from street lights or neighbors or traffic, and avoid any stimulation for the mind. Close curtains, pull shades, dim any lights.

AWE can become a ritual if you light some incense or candles. Or use a diffuser with essential oils such as frankincense or lavender, oils known to calm the mind and support a meditative state.

Light is a stimulant. Outside sound is a stimulant. Many scents are stimulants. Everything that comes in through your five or six senses has the potential to be a stimulant. The more that we can take stimulants out of the environment, the more we can tune into the inner environment. Where, then, is your cocoon? Somewhere nice and dark and warm and comfortable.

Meditation to Quiet Your Mind and the Ten Count

We start with a short meditation. Avoid the risk of falling back asleep, so please keep sitting up. I like to say that falling asleep while meditating is not meditation at all, but napitation. (Nothing wrong with a little napitation, just not before going into AWE.)

For the automatic writing experience, you don't have to be a great meditator. You don't have to be a yogini. You don't have to put yourself in the Himalayas or in a cave or be able to tremendously quiet your mind. All you need to do is slow things down. Just. A. Little. Bit.

Let me offer this simple ten-count meditation. It's perhaps the simplest, easiest meditation you'll ever do, and it's perfect for getting you into the automatic writing experience zone, getting you into that zone of AWE, as I like to call it.

Simple Ten-Count Meditation

Here's what you do. Simply breathe in nice and deeply through the nose, all the way down to the belly. You can even put a hand on your belly. And feel the belly expand. Then out through the nose. Again, in and out. That's called a ten count for a reason. You can find a video on this at www.AutomaticWriting.com/bonuses.

Breathe in and out, and think one. Breathe in and out, and think two.

Breathe in and out, and if you find your mind is thinking, "Oh, I forgot what I've got to take care of later today," breathe out again, and think one. And if you breathe in and out again and think, "Oh, wait, did I email that client?" That's one again as well.

In essence, each time you lose your train of thought and come back, that's a count of one. In theory you're trying to silence the mind and count to ten, but almost no one ever gets there. Instead, it's the one-two, cha-cha-cha. And there's no right or wrong here, or no such thing as a bad meditation.

Even if you end up going, one, two, one, one, one, one, one, that's perfect. For each time you catch your thoughts and bring yourself back, you're helping the mind detach from thought. And you're training your mind to get lighter, to get more still, and to uncouple from the whirling dervish of the monkey mind.

Basically, if you're focused on the breath, you add a count for each breath. Nobody ever gets to ten here, unless they're the Buddha. Some people may never make it to two for weeks. That's fine. If that's you, you're doing it right. You're strengthening the mindfulness muscles of your mind. You're strengthening that meditation center. Whether you get from one to three to five to ten, it doesn't matter. You're doing it perfectly well.

Five to ten minutes of this and you're ready to dive into AWE. Preferably ten minutes, but let's start where you are.

A note: Often beginners at meditation struggle to meditate for five to ten minutes, as time seems to grind by slowly, and there's an almost incessant need to check your watch. The simplest solution is to set a gentle, quiet, nonstimulating timer or alarm to alert you when you're done, then let it go. Forget about the time and simply fall into your ten count.

I learned another meditation technique from Claudio, my former meditation teacher on Maui who is now in Cozumel, Mexico. In his meditations, sitting in Tommy Bahama lounge chairs, the goal was to just totally be with whatever arose. In other words, to do nothing, to simply be with the chair and be with yourself, without effort or striving. As I like to joke, drooling is optional. You just simply be.

Thought comes up. "Oh." Another thought comes up. "Oh." No thought comes up. "Oh." No judgments. Just witness.

You just literally sit there not thinking about, not worrying about, not doing anything. That is the best meditation for this purpose to get ready for AWE, but it can be hard because the mind wants to go a thousand different directions, and if you haven't given yourself permission to just be, that can be the most challenging task in the world.

My recommendation: Do the ten count for ten minutes, and then if you feel like continuing, go into the silence. That's my favorite and what I recommend for clients as well. For it gives you the best of both worlds. First, you get to train your mind to observe and detach from your thoughts. And then you learn to savor the precious sweet silence. And to me, that's where the magic is.

The ten count is a way to keep you from hopping on the thought train each time the next train comes into the station. That's what we're working on here because we just don't want to stimulate the mind. This short meditation becomes a mindfulness practice for your entire day because you're actually training and working with the mind to learn how to not get on the train.

I like to tell my clients to think of a busy train station, or Penn Station in New York City. As you do your ten count, you'll accidentally find yourself on a train—perhaps it's the train labeled "work crisis" or "home crisis" or even "future vacation." It doesn't matter what the train is, when you find yourself accidentally on it, simply hop back off and go back into your meditation. This not only helps you with AWE, but can improve your concentration and reduce your anxiety throughout the day because you'll be more in control of your mind, worries, and concerns, rather than your thoughts being in charge of you.

To meditate, get comfortable. I encourage you to sit up nice and tall, but relaxed. Cross-legged on a cushion or seated in a chair are both fine. Many people like to sit in chairs and feel their feet on the floor.

No rules. The most important advice is being able to maintain your position for the duration of the meditation without feeling uncomfortable or continuously thinking about, or needing to adjust, your position. But other than that, any meditation is a perfect meditation.

As for how you meditate, as long as you don't use a tool like a recorded guided meditation, you're fine. A guided meditation in many ways actually stimulates the mind, so we want to stay in the silence. Therefore, if your butt hits the cushion, that's a perfect meditation. Again, no rules, whatever works for you.

Practice Nasal Breathing

Let me explain why we breathe through the nose with each inhalation and exhalation. Because such breathing doesn't trip the fight-or-flight mechanism in the nervous system.

You see, when we were babies, we would breathe through the nose if we wanted mama's milk or milk from the bottle. We were considered obligatory nasal breathers. And we were in bliss. However, when we had our first upper-respiratory infection, at some point we had a clogged nose and ended up gasping for breath, and we were breathing in through the mouth.

This mouth-breathing forced out of desperation, and still does, triggers a fight-or-flight response or a sympathetic nervous system response. Breathing through the mouth is what we do when we're running from tigers, and you can see it in other animals as well. That look of desperation when breathing from the mouth.

Conversely, breathing through the nose triggers a parasympathetic, or rest, relax, and digest response. When you're meditating, you definitely want to be in that state.

Avoid the Temptation to Turn on Your Phone

It is so easy to want to use a smartphone app for meditation. Please resist. First, a guided meditation stimulates the mind. And second, because while you're on your phone, you think, "Okay, I'll just check my email." Why? It's a habit. What kind of a habit? Like the open bag of potato chips on your desk, you'll eat half the bag before you realize it.

Don't give away your precious time and energy by opening your email or using your phone app for meditation right now. I've been calling email e-squared mail. What's that mean? It means it's every-one *else's* priorities or demands. Email is someone else's priorities that they're trying to get from you or take from you.

The more we can keep away from that energetic drain before writing, the better. Keep the phone in the other room if you don't need it for your brain-entrainment music (explanation coming up). And if you do have your phone nearby, then keep it on airplane mode and shut off those pings, whistles, beeps, and alerts. They give you a dopamine rush or hit at the very time you're working to go quiet.

Resist checking your email with everything you've got. For when you do your ten count or any other meditation after checking email, I guarantee you, you'll be thinking about the emails, what you need to do, or how you need to respond.

A wasp came into the studio not too long ago, and it kept banging its head against the ceiling, trying to get outside. It was worried and concerned and I could feel the energy—an energy of panic. I wanted to be able to rescue this creature and carry it out and give it a new chance at life. But it wouldn't stop moving and banging its head against the ceiling, so I couldn't catch it in a cup to take it out—until it relaxed, slowed down, and let go.

Our minds are often racing with ideas, worry, and anxiety. What about this? We ask. And what about that? The answers are always there. However, if we keep hitting our minds on the ceiling like the wasp, there's no way for us to slow down and hear what the Universe has to offer.

If that wasp had simply said, "I'm just going to do a ten count. I'm going to go sit on a windowsill and just be still for a while," something else would have come to him. In his case, the scoop of a glass and a lid, the proverbial hand of God, to take him outside.

That's the same with us in the morning preparing for AWE. We don't want to be the wasp because when the mind is racing, nothing can chase us down to help us get out of our current life circumstance.

Who Is in Your Environment?

Once you finish a short meditation, grab your favorite journal and a pen and hop over to a nice comfortable chair. At a little desk. Or at the kitchen table. Or don't move at all and continue the automatic writing experience in your cocoon. At this point, you should be in a complete state of relaxation.

If you set up to write at your home office desk, you may feel compelled to check email or feel the energetic imprint of work on that desk. AWE should not be work. It should not feel like work. If possible, don't do it where you do work.

You'll need enough light to see the pen and a little bit of what's on the page to make sure you're actually on the page. If your writing is really messy and gets ten times messier in automatic writing, it means you're doing it right. If you're challenged a bit in reading your writing later on, then you were in this half-here, half-not-here state. That's what we're looking for. And it's promoted and cultivated by having that darker cocoon-like environment.

If you have distractions in your environment, get them situated first. If the dog needs to go out, let the dog out. If the kitties demand to be fed, feed them. If the kids are making noise or the TV is on too loudly, consider going to bed even earlier and rising earlier to get your meditation and AWE in before they get up. And if you want to be a superstar at AWE, get up even before the fur babies.

If your environment is completely not conducive to doing your ritual, throw yourself out as early as you can and get yourself in a parked car, put in the earbuds for music, and do a quiet meditation. Then work to dive into AWE there. It's very challenging to do it in an environment where there's a hustle and bustle, which is why you want to go somewhere private. I've even had clients do this in a small closet, with clothes floating above them.

Just make sure wherever you go, you have some undisturbed time to write with as little movement around you as possible. If you just can't find solace and quiet in the morning, then consider doing AWE in the evening, after everybody goes to sleep. It's not ideal (as I discuss later in the book), but many people have had success doing AWE in the eve.

Your Secret Weapon: Binaural Theta Brain-Entrainment Music

I call it your secret weapon because for anyone who has struggled with automatic writing, brain-entrainment music seems to be a cure-all.

Once you move from meditation to your writing spot, you will put on binaural theta brain-entrainment music. All this ritual preparation has been to quiet your mind and get you where you are now going deeper into a theta brain wave state—where enlightenment takes place, or at least where you'll find words of wisdom.

Since I'm not a neuroscientist and don't play one on TV, I'm going to give you the layman's version of some science behind binaural brain-entrainment music. Pay attention, this may be a *Jeopardy!* question someday.

Binaural means you get a different sound coming into each ear—one side is aural, both sides is binaural. What happens when you get one sound coming from one side, another sound coming from the other side? Aha! The brain puts them together and basically links the left and right hemispheres or sides of the brain.

We get the left and right going together in sync, which leads to higher states of consciousness—and, more specifically, gets us out of that linear left brain and into the more creative or spiritual side. The linking can also lead to greater focus, greater concentration, and greater creativity. Many spectacular things can come out of having a different sound going to each ear at the same time. That's the binaural piece of it (pronounced *by-NOR-all*).

The other piece of this science lesson is the frequency, which refers to the soup we are swimming in—the quiet, dark environment for AWE.

If your apartment is in New York City, you're likely swimming in a steady soup of horns, car alarms, street sounds, and sirens. You then vibrate at the frequency of horns and sirens. If you live in a secluded mountain cabin with its peaceful solitude and bird chirps or a beach-front condo where you can hear gentle waves, then that's the frequency at which your mind vibrates as well.

With AWE, we want to get to a frequency where the mind is not highly focused, is not in a very idea-oriented place, but is in a plugged-in place of high creativity and receptivity coming beyond the thinking mind.

Specifically we want to go to a theta brain wave state. In this state we power down our executive functions or task-oriented parts of the brain—most specifically, the mid-prefrontal cortex, which does self-reflective "I, me, mine" thinking. We also power down the parietal lobe, which handles proprioception, which is the function of locating our bodies in space. When this powers down, we lose self-identification and feel connected to everything, or feel more connected to something greater than ourselves. These regions are part of what Dawson Church, PhD, calls the enlightenment circuit.

At this time we can feel really happy and we're connected with something greater than ourselves—in other words, beyond the egoic thinking mind. We enter a state Dr. Church calls "Bliss Brain."

Many, including myself, hypothesize and believe science will someday bear us out that as we enter this Bliss Brain state, we power up our pineal gland, also known as the third eye, which is famous for helping us reach the deepest or highest states of consciousness.

You can find interviews with both Dr. Church, author of *Bliss Brain: The Neuroscience of Remodeling Your Brain for Creativity, Resilience and Joy,* and Dr. Newberg, author of *How Enlightenment Changes the Brain* (written with Mark Robert Waldman), at our podcast's website (www.InspireNationShow.com).

If you want to touch heaven, you want to open up that pineal gland and power down that parietal lobe. That's where the action is. I explain the science behind this thinking in a later chapter. Actually, I call upon the experts to explain the science.

In a theta state, we are, therefore, shutting down the frontal lobe, the thinking part of our mind, and going to other regions of the brain, which are more connected to Source, connected to consciousness, or just connected to your inner wisdom—and your subconscious.

A lot of neuroscientists talk about lighting up the pineal gland for spiritual or enlightenment experiences that tend to come in a theta brain wave state. With AWE, we don't go fully to delta because that can also be sleep. We're going to one step before that—a theta brain wave state—where the mind is not trying to write letters. It's not trying to write emails, but where it is receptive and open to creativity coming to us.

BRAIN WAVE STATES

BETA — NORMAL LEVEL OF ALERTNESS. ALSO ASSOCIATED WITH STRESS, ANXIETY & FEAR.   14-30 HZ

ALPHA — CALM & PEACEFUL. CAN BE ACHIEVED THROUGH RELAXATION & LIGHT MEDITATION.   9-13 HZ

THETA — DEEP CREATIVE INSIGHT. FEELINGS OF ONENESS. ACHIEVED IN AUTOMATIC WRITING, DEEP MEDITATION & HYPNAGOGIC STATE.   4-8 HZ

DELTA — FOUND IN DEEP SLEEP. BEST FOR RENEWAL, HEALING, REJUVENATION, & RESTORING ONE'S IMMUNE SYSTEM.   .1-3 HZ

Human Brain Waves: The various human brain waves show the position of the theta waves in relation to other brain wave states.

In our stressed-out, high-anxiety, get-'er-done day-to-day world, we tend to live in a beta brain wave state. However kids before the age of seven naturally exist in this highly creative, intuitive plugged-in theta state. They're always on what I call both sides of the veil. They're both here in the thinking mind and in the heart. They're here in the physical realm. They're also on the spiritual side of things. They're able to tap into that inner wisdom and tap into their subconscious, which is why even a little smack on the hand to a two-year-old can become a trauma that can last through life because it goes straight into their subconscious.

The new science is showing that binaural music can help us tap into that realm of the theta brain waves. Whether you search YouTube for theta brain-entrainment music or download free music from our website, you can experiment with the sounds that work for you, whether it's seagulls or rain or something else (see www.AutomaticWriting.com/Bonuses).

If you're in a city and there's lots of street noise around you, you'll be able to create your cocoon with noise-canceling headphones so you don't have to listen to the blaring world around you. eBay and Amazon are likely sources for reasonably priced headphones, but, of course, buy local if you can. If your environment is reasonably quiet, then less cumbersome AirPods or earbuds are fine.

There are several benefits to wearing headphones or earbuds over listening to ambient sound from speakers in front of you or coming from an iPad or iPod. Remember the binaural discussion, with different sounds coming in each side.

Putting your headphones on brings the sound right into your head. Not only are you protected from the sounds around you, in a sense, but you are making it easier for your brain to entrain to that music, to get in sync or in tune with the frequency of that music.

Is the music absolutely necessary? No. I don't want you to think that you need it or that it's a crutch and you won't be able to do automatic writing without it. But I found that using theta brain-entrainment music has led to some profound experiences for me, and especially for those that I coach. The music gets them from entering the on-ramp straight to the fast lane—just like that.

And for those who used to struggle with automatic writing, simply adding the brain-entrainment music, while changing nothing else, often solved the problem.

You have now:

1. Taken care of the bare minimum early-morning chores,
2. Meditated in your quiet cocoon for a minimum of ten minutes using the ten count or another meditation,

3. Moved to a quiet place where you can write,

4. Chosen theta brain-entrainment music to further quiet your mind and turn off the thinking part,

5. Put in your earbuds or noise-canceling headphones, and now

6. You are ready to call upon the Universe for an AWE-some experience.

3 | How to Begin Words and Prayers to Get You Going

A s you start to put pen to paper, I have created a few ways to get your brain (and pen) engaged in the process. We start with an intention prayer, an invocation prayer, and then questions to engage our guides.

Your Intention Prayer

The intention prayer is the first (written) step in automatic writing and opening yourself up to your deepest wisdom. I like to think of the intention prayer as helping you create a bubble of love and light from which to write, or the sacred vessel that encapsulates you and helps you call in the words. From a purely functional perspective, it's like the first step down the rabbit hole and into the unknown. If we considered the automatic writing experience (AWE) like shamanic journeying, it'd be starting up the drums and heading down into the underworld—the place where magic and guides await.

When I work with my clients, I always ask if they pray to God or a god, Source, Universe, a higher self, inner wisdom, Jesus, Buddha,

Allah, or whomever (out of complete and total respect). You can write to any of these in your intention prayer. I simply recommend going to the highest source you can. I'm going to take you to the highest level of your religious belief and that's where we're going to call in the information.

I'm going to share with you what works for me and what works for many of my coaching clients and those who have gone through my online AWE course. But feel free to use whatever works for you. If you're secular, or atheist, feel free to simply write to your inner wisdom. AWE will work no matter what. And, yes, you get to bring your spiritual and religious beliefs to the practice. That's what's most important—do what works and feels most comfortable for you.

Automatic writing is totally inclusive, so will work with anything, but I recommend you bring in all of your beliefs. Let's not keep that at the door. That's coming from your heart at this point. That's where the answers are going to come from as well.

For myself, I write to God in my prayers, though I do not believe in a bearded white guy, or anything like it, in the sky. Instead God to me refers to the love we came from and the love that we are, or as Dr. Ervin Laszlo, two-time Nobel Peace Prize nominee (and repeat guest on our show), refers to it as the Akashic field, the field of love and information that affirms and informs everything. It is the energy we are surrounded by, filled up with, and that literally makes our very existence. That's what God is to me.

If you would rather not consider this a prayer or appeal to a god or God, you can replace the word *God* that I use here. Even that giant cheeseburger in the sky, I've referred to, so make your intention known to whomever or whatever works for you.

Basically, in this step, you are setting the table with your intention for the automatic writing to flow. Feel free to modify as need be.

Whether you've done this a hundred times or a thousand, write out your intention prayer. I use the acronym G-S-P-I (pronounced jē-spī) to recall the words. Here's what I write:

Thank you, God, for **guiding** me with your love and light.

Thank you, God, for **surrounding** me with your love and light.

Thank you, God, for **protecting** me with your love and light.

Thank you, God, for **imbuing** me with your love and light.

Thank you, God. Thank you, God. Thank you, God.

A completely secular version could be this:

Thank you, Inner Wisdom, for **guiding** me with your love and light.

Thank you, Inner Wisdom, for **surrounding** me with your love and light.

Thank you, Inner Wisdom, for **protecting** me with your love and light.

Thank you, Inner Wisdom, for **imbuing** me with your love and light.

Thank you, Inner Wisdom. Thank you, Inner Wisdom. Thank you, Inner Wisdom.

I equate the automatic writing experience we call AWE to dating. You start with a handshake. You get to know this inner wisdom. You get to develop a relationship. You start to get to know each other. You cultivate this relationship. When you water the seeds, you see them grow.

That process takes time and commitment. I ask for you to give the process thirty days of continuous practice, every day. Thirty days. During that time, just as you enjoy getting to know new friends, perhaps over coffee or a walk, through AWE, you get to know yourself.

If you make the commitment to date yourself in a sense for thirty days, everything changes. Now, does your entire life change? In many ways, actually, it does because if you haven't had a process to tap into your inner wisdom and you keep up with it for thirty days, you will feel better, lighter, and supported, and you will feel more on track. Of course, you may not have the answers to all of life's deepest questions . . . yet.

But you're going to say, "Wow, I've got a GPS. I have an idea of how to get where I want to go, or, more likely, I get to figure out where I want to go." That comes from the practice and the repetition.

Most importantly, like dating, you don't typically go from a quick hello online straight to bed. Okay, it's a changing world, but this is dating, not a hookup. If you move too quickly in AWE, you lose the connection. Instead, cultivate the relationship and get comfortable with the basics before you move on to the big questions.

I start out with little bits and pieces with just three basic questions, which I'll get to in a moment. Then we start to blow things out more. And more. Then we add some manifestation techniques and some visualization techniques and some dreaming techniques, and even some finance techniques. Then, after thirty days, you're going to say, "Wow, I've got some real tools to work with."

Our opening intention prayer, then, is both creating your vessel of love and light and a connection to your inner wisdom. You are creating your sacred internal space to write just as you have created your sacred environment externally.

Your Invocation Prayer

Now that you've done your intention prayer and set the table, it's time to invoke or invite in that inner wisdom or guidance so that the words can flow. This is what we call our invocation prayer or our welcoming-in prayer.

I share with you the words that I use, and understand that I am kind of woo-woo about this. But you should call in whomever, whatever you want, or simply your inner wisdom.

You can think of this as calling in your team or board of directors, which is similar to what Napoleon Hill described in his book *Think and Grow Rich*. He called in numerous historical figures for his automatic writing, and even a few live figures such as Thomas Edison. Apparently, these characters would even have disagreements in his writing. And as for Thomas Edison, Napoleon once approached him and asked him about comments he'd gotten from Edison in his writing—and Edison didn't disagree.

I have a large team I like to call in, and it morphs from day to day. Sometimes I'm calling in the whole team, or sometimes someone specifically. For instance, to protect our house and our land, I'll call in Mother Earth, or Mother Nature, the spirit of the land, elders, and a mountain lion I've seen on the property, quite literally, and written to in AWE, whose spirit goes by the name of Maximilian.

I also like to call on three elders who've crossed over to the other side (more on this later). They are my best man, Jack, who was eighty-nine years young at the time of our wedding and didn't retire from his last job driving around the "youngsters" (the seventy and eighty-year-olds in the nursing home bus) until he was ninety-two. There's our spiritual *kupuna* from Maui, Auntie Pua, who taught us about the spirit of aloha. And our dear, dear friend Carla, who crossed over just two years ago. I tend to call each of them in on a regular basis.

Lastly I like to call in our pet Nacho Molé, our baby vole whom we literally nursed with a bottle from the age of four days—Jessica did the majority of the feeding—and passed away far too young. I call him in regularly from the other side. While Jack will always give me a nudge or a kick in the pants if he feels I get off track, Molé is always encouraging me and giving me the best pep talks.

Think of who you feel is by your side, or a dear loved one who passed away, or perhaps even a spirit or spiritual figure that visited you in your dreams. Sometimes I write to Harry S. Truman, strange as it seems, after he once visited me in a dream. I haven't learned anything particularly interesting from him yet, but who knows? And then there's my grandmother on my mother's side. She keeps coming in, wanting to have a talk.

As I mentioned earlier, I'm an angels guy, meaning I'm always calling in angels and the archangels. In fact, when I share the intention prayer with my coaching clients, I always ask, "Are you down with the archangels?" because other than adding in Mother Earth or Mother Nature, the angels seem to be the most important place to start.

So if you're down with the archangels, call them in. And if not, no worries as well. But if you're into angels, I believe they're always with us, always willing to lend a helping hand, but in other than life-or-death situations, they won't intervene unless we call on them.

Here's how the basic invocation prayer goes and feel free to modify any way you wish. This is my abridged version, so feel free to call in your whole team.

This is my invocation prayer:

> Good morning, Mother Earth, Mother Nature.
> Good morning, Archangel Michael, Archangel Raphael,
>   Archangel Gabriel.
> Good morning, higher self, higher team, and all angels,
>   guides, and light workers here for my highest good and
>   the highest good of all.

That's basically it. For my personal team, I add:

> Good morning, Jack. Good morning, Carla. Good morning,
> Auntie Pua. Good morning, Molé. Good morning, Maximil-
> ian. Thank you for protecting our home and the land. Good
> morning, spirits of the land, spiritual elders, ancestors, and
> all angels, guides, and light workers, here for my highest good
> and the highest good of all.

And I'm even known for adding in my microbiome, something I first heard of from a coaching client in Holland. Since there are perhaps trillions of micro-organisms in our body, why not include them, for they are us.

Please note, you can even call in living beings. Meaning, if you want to connect with the spirit of a leader, an artist, a scientist, or anyone else, you can simply call them in. Will they respond? Well, that's up to them.

A secular version may be this one:

> Good morning, energy. Good morning, love. Good morning,
> inner wisdom. Good morning, higher self [that's simply your
> inner spirit]. Good morning, Earth. Good morning, sky. Good
> morning, day. Good morning, sunshine.

On the following page is a page from one practitioner's journal she kindly shared with us so you can see her invocation prayer:

> AWE
> Day 1
>
> Le 24 décembre 2018
>
> Good morning Higher Self, Higher Team.
> Good morning inner wisdom.
> Good morning inner guidance.
> Good morning inner voice.
>
> God thank you for guiding me with
> your love & light.
>
> God thank you for surrounding me
> with your love & light.
>
> God thank you for imbuing me with
> your love & light.
>
> God thank you for protecting me
> with your love & light.
>
> Thank You.
> Thank You.
> Thank You.

Note the invocation prayer written out in this practitioner's journal.

Once you have written your invocation prayer, then you're ready for question number one.

Ask the First Question: What do I need to know today?

After you've written out your invocation prayer, dive immediately into your first question, do not pause, nor pass go. Immediately write out, "What do I need to know today," and now, for the next five to ten minutes, do not stop writing.

Here's the key: write gibberish if you have to, but do not think about what to write. Lately I've been joking and telling people to write stupid. In other words, don't ask your mind what to write, but simply keep the pen flowing.

If you've heard of free writing, this part of automatic writing is a bit similar, in that you write whatever comes to you without regard to spelling, grammar, or logic, and here's the most important part, you write without stopping. That means do not stop to make corrections, analyze what you've written, or judge the contents of your writing.

Don't worry at all about what's coming out of your head or where this is coming from for this five to ten minutes. Just let the pen and the words flow. This part of the process is designed to loosen your mind's grip on the critical nature of writing and to move past any potential resistance such as fear and anxiety, control or self-criticism.

You might want to write *I don't know what to write, I don't know what to write* or you might simply repeat your prayers, *good morning, good morning, good morning.* Whatever you do, just simply keep the pen flowing without thought.

Many beginners to automatic writing will experience performance anxiety: fear that they will fail at the process. The fear can be so great that they never even begin. The irony is that fear and anxiety are often to blame for stifled writing. Just do your best to let go of the outcome. Expect a lot of useless, throw-away writing in the beginning—that's by design. Later on that writing becomes interspersed with pearls of wisdom. And with even more dedicated practice, you'll find even less writing to toss and more to hold near and dear to your heart.

What will typically happen, though, is another stream of consciousness will sneak in while you are writing: I don't know what to write. I don't know what to write. *This is silly. Why am I doing this? It's going to be all right, Michael. I don't know what to write. I don't know what to write. You are loved. I don't know what to write, I don't know what to write. Relax. Everything is perfect. I don't know what to write, I don't know what to write. The words are gonna flow. You don't have to worry about it. You're going to have a beautiful day. I don't know what to write.*

Words just seem to come in tiny snippets at first, and it's not important what's coming out, it just means you've started a cosmic handshake or connection with your inner wisdom.

Key caveat: In the past I would tell coaching clients to put pen to paper and, for the next five to ten minutes, don't pick up the pen, no matter what. And they took me literally. So a clarification, it's okay to cross your t's or dot your i's. If not, it's hard to tell what in the world you've actually written. Feel free to pick up the pen between words. Instead, what I do mean is don't stop writing.

With that said, if your writing is almost unintelligible when you review it afterward, that's actually a sign. It means that you were in a place of writing without thought and that's perfect, keep it up. And at some point, some third-person wisdom sneaks in. In fact, that's how you know it's the automatic writing experience. The words are not coming out in your writing voice. Just keep writing. When that happens, don't worry about where the words are coming from or whether you're doing it right or not.

Just keep the pen flowing: *I don't know what to write. I don't know what to write. I have no idea why I'm doing this. My mind is completely blank.* If your mind is truly completely blank, congratulations. You've reached enlightenment. You're the Buddha. But whatever is coming up, just keep writing. Don't worry if things come up or if they don't.

I like to think of this process as an airplane taking off. In fact, that's kind of a general theme through this whole program. In the beginning, you'll start to get a few words. The airplane starts gaining speed down the runway. You start to get a little lift. Then you start to analyze what you're writing, and the plane comes back down. You start to get a few more words. You're getting a little bit more into AWE, and the plane starts to lift again. Then you judge your handwriting, critique the writing, or even correct spelling or grammar mistakes, and the plane comes back down again.

That's okay. You're learning how to take flight. This process takes time. It could take a few days. It could take a few weeks. It's rare that it takes you longer than a month, but I've had one or two discouraged coaching clients who stuck with it, and I'm so glad they did because their practice took off after three months. And most importantly, they felt much better through the process. For it's as much energetic as it is verbal. This means that you're often making a powerful energetic handshake with the Universe or your inner wisdom, far before the words come through.

Everyone can access AWE. If you've ever turned the car at the last second to avoid a hazard, or picked up the phone to call someone, and they were already on the other end, then you've tapped into AWE. It's always there for you, waiting. No matter what, something profound is going to come out of this for you.

As you work to take off and stay aloft, you're training your mental muscles. You're helping yourself to be able to hear better—on the inside. So even if you're not getting profound words of wisdom in the beginning, you're getting something out of it. I share more about attuning to a higher frequency through AWE in a later chapter.

One of the top questions, perhaps the number-one question, is where is this writing coming from? If it's a kind, gentle, patient, loving voice, then that's the voice of AWE.

But if you're getting shoulda, woulda, coulda, or feeling your AWE is "should-ing" all over yourself, that's not your higher self. That's not your inner wisdom. That's your ego speaking to you. That's okay too. We can work with this, and this voice can even help you.

While you might be focused mentally on, "Oh, my God. I've got this problem with my job, with my finances, with my wife, with my child," those may seem to be your most pressing concerns. Your inner wisdom, however, may have something else that it needs to address with you first, and we need to give it that opportunity.

So when ego comes up, I suggest you picture a giant Thunderbird convertible, perhaps similar to the car in *Thelma & Louise,* with white leather seats. Then you're simply going to ask ego to take a backseat, as far away from you as possible.

Let ego know you'll be back to her, or back to him, and it's only for a few minutes. In this way, ego will let you hear your inner wisdom, before you give ego time. However, you must make sure to come back to ego. For you need to keep your word.

If you're getting negative berating with *I should have done this* or *I could have done that,* ask your ego to put that on a back burner and you'll take care of that later. (In a chapter addressing AWE questions about technique, I address how to take advantage of this ego speak and how to use it to heal emotional wounds and blocks.)

So when ego steps up, stop. Take a brief pause. Recognize that's your ego. Tell ego you're going to write about the ego later and go right back to *I don't know what to write. I have no idea what I'm writing* until something else pops up.

Janet, an AWE student of mine, is herself a psychotherapist. When she asks the question, "What do I need to know today," she said she finds herself feeling as if she's getting a daily therapy session for free. She said, "It feels good to have my time in meditation and automatic writing so that I hear my inner voice and my feelings each morning as I start my day."

Another practitioner shared this page from his journal when he wrote, *What do I need to know for today?*

When one practitioner wrote, *What do I need to know for today?*
this is what AWE told him.

Ask the Second Question: Who am I?

After five to ten minutes, it's time to move on to the second, perhaps most profound question you'll ever ask yourself. This question helps you get to know yourself on the deepest soul level. Three simple words. The most important question to ask yourself is this: "Who am I?"

Then put the pen to paper again and for the next five to ten minutes, let it flow. Don't worry, don't think, and don't try to answer the question. Again, this is really asking on a global perspective who you are, not about you simply being a parent, or what your job is, or any of the day-to-day definitions of who you see yourself to be. For this is not coming from you.

See what comes to you. Often at first, you're going to write this: *I'm not sure what to write. What do I write here? I don't know what to write. Who am I? Who am I? Who am I?* Again in the beginning, all we're looking for is a glimpse, just a few words to come through. Often, though, this question is quite profound, and you get a lot more than a few words fairly quickly. This is one of those game-changing or life-changing questions because when you start to get an answer to this—a glimpse of who you truly are and why you're truly here—it helps to change everything.

I recommend you do this each time you go to your automatic writing for the first few weeks. After that we can change out this question for ones of inquiry—more on this in a later chapter as well.

I like to think of this question as looking at a gemstone. Each time you ask this question, you are getting an answer from a different facet of the precious stone. One day you're going to get one answer to the question, and on another day, you'll see another facet of that answer. All of these visions add up to make the gemstone of you, something very rich and three-dimensional. Enjoy.

Ask the Third Question: What's my SMP?

Now that you've asked the first question: "What do I need to know today?" And you've successfully asked the second question, "Who am I?" it's time to ask one more question to set up your day for success.

Why a third question? While you're hopefully starting to tap into your inner wisdom, to develop a relationship with your higher self, you might be wondering how is that relevant in the following moments and hours and the day ahead? This third question helps with that.

It's what I call the "chop wood, carry water" question, as in, before enlightenment, chop wood, carry water—after enlightenment, chop wood, carry water.

So to find out what kind of chopping wood and carrying water for the day (tasks) you're going to be doing, you're going to write this: *What's my SMP—my single-minded purpose?* or *What's the single most important task or thing I get to do today?*

In essence, this question helps you know what's the one most important thing to get done today, that if you got it done, then if nothing else gets done, everything is great. It's not an answer coming from the head and isn't a to-do list. It could be two or three items, instead of an SMP, but if it's more than that, then it's clearly a to-do list from the head.

The funny thing is, the answers are rarely what you think they'll be. It might be to respond to an email, or that you forgot to pay a bill (it's rather handy when the Universe reminds you of this), but it might be something entirely different.

For myself, for the longest time, almost until 2020, nine out of ten times I'd get the same SMP each and every day, "Take better care of the Pookie" (my nickname for Jessica). The guides apparently have my number. The better I take care of her, then no matter what else happens, it's a great day.

That SMP did change in the beginning of 2020 to one of slowing down and relaxing more, and that completely morphed once COVID-19 came about. Now it's all about recharging, refilling my tanks, and leaving fuel in reserve for whatever's coming next.

So after your first two questions, let's get that third question going, "What's my SMP?" And then put pen to paper and write without thought. I can't emphasize this enough, because it's easy to go to a to-do list with this question.

Now while AWE might give you two or three tasks as your single-minded purpose, it's not unheard of if you get more than that. Then rest assured it's a to-do list from your egoic mind, not from AWE. Write down the answer that flows through and then take action on that purpose later in the day.

The next section instructs you how to review your automatic writing later in the same day. Your answer to this question acts as a reminder that you have a single-minded purpose.

Here's a tip: Once you've completed your AWE for the morning, write down your SMP on a sticky note, index card, or take a photo of your writing in your journal on your phone. Then set a reminder to look at the message later in the day.

AWE is not about hard work, it's about developing a relationship, like dating, with your inner wisdom, higher self, or whatever you'd like to call it, but in the kindest and gentlest fashion you can. For me, that means playing, having fun with things, and seeing what comes up.

Then of course, it's time to get up from that chair, stretch those legs, and get some movement or breakfast (or, if you're writing at night, it's time for bed).

How Do I Start a Dialogue with My Guides?

Just to clarify, when I talk about my guides, I could be referring to your inner wisdom, your higher self, your spirit guides, angels, or whatever higher intelligence you wish to connect with.

At this point, I highly recommend checking out the 30-Day Challenge in chapter 14. With that said, after you have been practicing automatic writing for a few weeks, asking yourself the first question (What do I need to know today?), the second question (Who am I?), and your third question (What's my single-minded purpose?), it's time to start a dialogue with your inner self.

For the first few weeks I recommend that you keep all three questions just as is. However, once the words are flowing, it becomes redundant to ask who am I day after day after day. So I'd recommend after a few weeks of getting answers to the who am I question, switch it out for deeper questions about yourself, about life, or really about anything.

This middle question is your opportunity to learn about yourself and life or literally have the equivalent of a conversation with God. For myself, this is my opportunity to talk with my inner wisdom, or Universe, or even a particular angel or guide, and ask anything and everything. Such as why is COVID-19 happening? Are we supposed to travel? Why did we have three miscarriages—and what can we learn from them? There's nothing that's not on the table.

Here are some of the different questions you can ask. And I recommend going off-script as well. Don't be afraid to ask topical questions that have the most meaning for you:

- What's my purpose?
- Am I on track?
- Should I stay or should I go?
- How do I shed the fears and worries I'm facing today?
- What is going on (with a particular situation)?
- Why does this pattern keep repeating?

Ask anything and everything you can think of. Here are more prompts:

- How do I get a better job, or should I stay at my current position?
- How do I improve my relationship?
- Is there a better way that I can communicate with my daughter, son, or parent/s?
- How do I resolve a conflict with my coworkers or boss?
- What's the answer to this big decision I need to make?
- How do I increase my income or grow my business?
- Where in the world do I move?
- What do I need to know about this pandemic or national crisis?

As I mentioned earlier, if instead of beautiful, deep, supportive words of wisdom, negativity starts coming up or you get shoulda, woulda, couldas from these questions, that's not AWE but your ego speaking. If this is the case, I discuss ego in the next section, where I suggest writing down the message and shredding it, then going back to AWE.

Don't expect too much in your early weeks. You're really just starting to make a handshake or a connection between you and your higher self, your inner wisdom or the Divine. So no matter how slowly it goes, you're right on track making that connection. You're literally building new neural pathways and spirit pathways. In fact, over time, the voice grows so strong inside of you that you can hear it anytime, without even needing a pen, or feel the words of wisdom—*even when you're not writing.*

The Ego Dump

Here's a powerful exercise that will allow you to let ego's voice help heal you and integrate those pieces creeping into your AWE. Consider that everything that's coming up is actually here to serve you. It's not off course, it's not off path, it *is* the path.

This is going to sound completely sacrilegious if you've ever done any law of attraction or New Thought work or anything of the sort or follow Rhonda Byrne's *The Secret*.

You might think, what I think about I bring about. And if I write out the negative, that's exactly what I'll get. But instead, if you don't get it up and out, you'll likely have a volcano on your hands or get quite sick. So we need to get whatever's inside of you up and out.

So write down every single negative word your ego has to say with you or say to you. Barf them all out. I call this exercise either the Ego Dump or the Better Out than In because everything that you stuff inside of you will either eat you alive mentally, spiritually, or psychologically, or turn into illness or injury. I speak from personal experience too, particularly with my past back pain.

Don't be ashamed. Don't be embarrassed. Don't censor yourself. If there's self-loathing, there's anger, there's a desire to hit yourself in the gut—and I've really been there, quite literally, then get it all out on paper. If it's judging you, get it out. If you feel you screwed up, get it out. If you feel worthless, get it out no matter what it is. Let ego have her or his say.

In this case, it's not what you think about, you bring about. It's what you stuff inside of you that comes back with a vengeance, or becomes a seething volcano inside of you.

After you've written your Ego Dump, you need to do the next step (which is why I don't recommend typing this out on a keyboard). Take that piece of paper and shred it. Burn it. And be done with it.

Why? Because your subconscious doesn't know the difference between the written word and an actual event or emotion, by writing it out, and tearing it up, you help purge it out of your system.

You may have to do this a bunch of times, but each time you do, you'll feel lighter and lighter still. Of course, I wouldn't do this exercise unless the negativity or egoic mind comes up during AWE; if so, you can do this daily, but if not, I'd leave it alone. AWE will let you know when it's time to warm up the paper shredder.

Make these Ego Dumps into a ritual. You could write, *Archangel Michael, Archangel Rafael, Archangel Gabriel, higher self, higher team, and all angels, guides and light workers, here for my highest good and the highest good of all,* (or simply *Dear Inner Wisdom*) *please help me to heal these wounds once and for all.* Then shred and shred and shred.

Now while you're asking them to be gone once and for all, they may come back at a deeper level on another day. But each time you are getting healthier and lighter for getting it out. This is part of integrating the ego by allowing ego to have its say. Never push it away.

Never say, "No, this is about automatic writing. I'm not going to go to that negative place because what you think about is what you're bringing up." No. Go there. Know that you're loved and supported and know that whatever you are writing through automatic writing has got your back, so you're in a beautiful, sacred space from which to do this incredibly powerful healing work. There's an angelic expression, ask and ye shall receive. So if you need to, ask the angels, ask your guides, or simply your inner wisdom to support you, guide you, heal you, and even comfort you through this process.

Close with Gratitude

People often ask me if I close my automatic writing down after I finish so I can go about my day. And to me, I say just the reverse. I want the AWE portal open throughout the day so I can hear the words more clearly, when I need them most—in the thick of things.

However, while I don't shut down AWE at the end of each session, I do express my gratitude. For I feel the more gratitude I bring to
AWE, the more it helps bring good things about. And so, when I finish
my AWE, no matter how long or how short the session, I'll thank the
angels, my inner wisdom, guides, Source, Universe, and anyone and
anything I believe I may have been writing to.

Quick Start Guide and Reminder Sheet

1 | Meditate for five to ten minutes (use the ten count if you wish or sit in silence). Move to your writing spot or stay where you are and put on your theta brain wave entrainment music.

2 | Intention Prayer (remember G-S-P-I), get your journal and pen and write:

> Thank you, God [or your higher power of choice], for guiding me with your love and light.
> Thank you, God, for surrounding me with your love and light.
> Thank you, God, for protecting me with your love and light.
> Thank you, God, for imbuing me with your love and light.
> Thank you, God. Thank you, God. Thank you, God.

Or the secular version could be this:

> Thank you, Inner Wisdom, for guiding me with your love and light.
> Thank you, Inner Wisdom, for surrounding me with your love and light.
> Thank you, Inner Wisdom, for protecting me with your love and light.
> Thank you, Inner Wisdom, for imbuing me with your love and light.
> Thank you, Inner Wisdom. Thank you, Inner Wisdom. Thank you, Inner Wisdom.

3 | Invocation Prayer (modify as you wish) and write:

Good morning, Mother Earth, Mother Nature.

Good morning, Archangel Michael, Archangel Raphael, Archangel Gabriel.

Good morning, higher self, higher team, and all angels, guides, and light workers here for my highest good and the highest good of all.

For my personal team, I add:

Good morning, Jack. Good morning, Carla. Good morning, Auntie Pua. Good morning, Molé. Good morning, Maximilian. Thank you for protecting our home and the land. Good morning, spirits of the land, spiritual elders, ancestors, and all angels, guides, and light workers, here for my highest good and the highest good of all.

A secular version may be this one:

Good morning, energy. Good morning, love. Good morning, inner wisdom. Good morning, higher self [that's simply your inner spirit]. Good morning, Earth. Good morning, sky. Good morning, day. Good morning, sunshine.

4 | The First Questions, write the first question and then the second and the third (about five to ten minutes for each):

What do I need to know today?

Who am I?

What's my SMP?

5 | Close with Gratitude

4 | The Best Time of Day for Automatic Writing

A n entire chapter devoted to the best time for doing your AWE (automatic writing experience)? Why, yes! I would be doing you a disservice if I didn't include a compelling argument for doing your AWE first thing in the morning. I'll begin by explaining why first thing in the morning gives you the best chance for success. Then I'll give you some tips for your evenings that will make it a lot easier for you to wake up bright eyed and bushy tailed and looking forward to your AWE session.

By the time we're through with this chapter, perhaps you will be convinced to either get up a wee bit earlier or at a bare minimum to carve out a little time for AWE during your existing morning routine.

For myself, out of all the self-help tips before discovering AWE, rising early was the one that made the greatest impact in my life, and the one I railed against the most. Whether it was Stephen Covey, or any of a plethora of amazing self-help authors and gurus, I resisted that one pivotal technique—the early rise. That was, until I read Robin Sharma's *The Monk Who Sold His Ferrari*. For whatever reason, that book clicked, and this former night owl gave it a try. And it changed everything.

Why Early Mornings
Are Best for AWE

First, automatic writing helps set us up for the best possible day ahead. Second, our ability to access our deepest wisdom changes depending on the time of day. One way to look at it is the farther the sun is below the horizon (before sunrise), the deeper the words of wisdom you're going to get. There seem to be two key reasons for this.

When the sun's far down below the horizon, at least depending on the time of year, people around you are asleep. And as quantum physics now shows, we're all one, all connected by and a part of a giant energetic field. You can call it a quantum field, or the Akashic field, or simply love. But when this field of energy is sleeping, then it's easiest to get your deepest words of wisdom. And when it's awake, it's quite difficult to write anything too profound.

If you've ever flown over a major metropolis at night, you've seen a field of light down below, entire cities or landscapes transformed by light. It's an easy way to think of the field of energy we're all swimming in. We're all swimming in the light of others around us. However, instead of light, think of this energy as psychic; in this field are everyone's worries, fears, and concerns.

Now early in the morning, this light is faint, as people are still sleeping and so, too, are their worries. So early in the morning, when the sun is far below the horizon, it's incredibly easy to get deep words of wisdom. But as the sun comes up, and people wake up, so do their concerns. And the more that's on their minds, the more that'll be on yours.

As an example, Jessica and I used to live in New Jersey, just outside of New York City. In the early-morning hours I could dive deep into

AWE, hearing about her health, starting our show, and even about my coaching business. But then, around 6:00 a.m., or perhaps even earlier, things would start to change. I'd have a hard time diving deep, but instead would almost get a to-do list in my automatic writing.

What was going on? Before 6:00, the world around me slept. But then, people woke, and started whizzing past our neighborhood trying to beat the traffic into New York City. In essence, the field was waking up and getting ready for their commute—and there was so much "noise" in the air, psychically, that it became impossible to dive deep. Instead I could feel their fear and worries, which led to a giant to-do list.

Now there's nothing wrong with hearing in AWE what you get to do, but that's not really the primary intention. However, as the sun comes up, we do get more of the chop wood, carry water answers. The expression comes from a popular zen quote: "Before Enlightenment, chop wood, carry water. After Enlightenment, chop wood, carry water." In other words, once people are in a get-'er-done mentality, that's where your automatic writing goes too.

Therefore, your holiest messages, so to speak, come at the holier hours, the times when the rest of the world is sleeping. Loosely speaking, I tend to consider the holy hour 4:00 a.m. to 6:00 a.m. (even though it's a two-hour span). But consistently that seems to be the time that people get their deepest, most profound wisdom from AWE.

If you work night shifts and your sleep cycle is different, no problem. Just do AWE when you awaken in a half-awake state, preferably late at night when the rest of the world sleeps. And if not, simply do the best you can and find a quiet cocoon.

My student Linda shares her practice:

> My best place to practice AWE is sitting up in a spot with only
> natural light coming in since I have found my best time to

practice AWE writing is around 6:15 a.m. I have tried different times earlier, but my body is not as willing to get into it as I can around the natural time I wake up and it's still early enough to be quiet as well as low natural lighting, sun having just started peeking up just after sunrise.

Just this morning I had a name come to me while practicing AWE: Linda Lou. I stopped and thought, that's Aunt Karen. The only person that ever called me by that fun nickname, she would always get a kick out of saying it and would give a little smile whenever she would say it. She was always playful and young at heart and passed over twenty years ago. I've never felt her before but thought that I will include her into my starting prayer and invocation from now on.

How Does My Sleep Routine and Bedtime Make a Difference?

When I teach my coaching clients automatic writing, I ask when they go to sleep. Why? Because sleep and your sleep routine may be key to a successful automatic writing experience. Let's look at your sleep routine and examine how your sleep may be improved with AWE.

Often people come to me and say, "Michael, I'd love to do automatic writing, or I'd love to do it first thing in the morning, but I just can't find the time." The secret to finding the time isn't about seeing what fits in your existing schedule. It's about rearranging your schedule, changing habits, and committing to *making* the time. And this process starts the night before.

During the night before, create a wind-down routine. For instance, set alarms to alert you to when you need to start winding things down.

I tend to have people set an alarm one hour before bedtime, to make sure they're winding down, and a second alarm fifteen minutes before bedtime to let them know it's time to go to bed.

What does winding down look like? It could be dimming the lights and turning off the electronics an hour before bedtime. It could be using candles. Or incense or gentle music. It's about setting markers for your body, mind, and soul that tell you it's time to wind down. It's typically getting away from the news and other stimulating activities, even an exciting book—conversely, a boring book could be perfect for helping you fall asleep.

Whatever you do, make sure it's a positive activity because whatever you feed your mind before you go to sleep will also feed your subconscious while you sleep. I cannot state this enough. Zombie movies, zombie news, or reading about the latest politician or political scandal will not help you while you sleep. Your mind is a creation machine, so whatever you focus on is what you bring about. Make sure it's something positive. For that's what your mind will work on for the next six to eight or more hours.

I recommend not eating hours before bedtime because eating stimulates your digestive system, which stimulates your internal fire, which keeps you awake. And I highly recommend, if at all possible, following the Ayurvedic principle of getting to bed before 10:00 p.m.— even earlier, if you can.

In regard to sleep, Dr. Kapil Shripad Apshankar, a student of AWE, said, "When I practice AWE before sleep, I almost always surrender the things that did not work out for me through the day to the Divine. I convert these into questions, and I typically get my answers the following morning or in the next couple of days."

Set a 10:00 p.m. Bedtime

Medical science knows getting to bed is essential for a deep night's sleep. It's something that's been written about in the ancient medical wisdom of Ayurveda for the last 5,000-plus years.

If you think of the body as being a furnace, that furnace gets hotter and colder throughout the day. The first cycle comes up to burn food, then goes down to rest, then comes up to digest again, and then down again, and it comes up after 10:00 p.m., like a preset oven cleaning, to help remove toxins and waste from your digestive system and from your mind. It's a built-in purification system for the body.

This inner flame kicks back up just after 10:00 p.m. If we get to bed before then, we tend to wake far more rested and refreshed. However, if we stay up after 10:00, we start to become exceptionally awake, wired, and hungry. In fact, after 10:00, our hormones switch so that the hormone that makes us hungry, ghrelin, gets stuck on, and the hormone that regulates satiation or makes us full, leptin, goes off. This means that after 10:00 it's almost a guarantee you'll get the munchies, and no matter how many leftovers you consume while standing in front of the open refrigerator, you'll never be satisfied.

Interestingly, this cycle doesn't just go for food after 10:00 at night, it goes for other stimulation as well. For instance, no matter how much you surf the web after 10:00, you're never satisfied. Or no matter how many episodes of *Game of Thrones*, or your latest Netflix binge is, you're never satisfied. Now this wouldn't be so bad if we were focused on work after 10:00, but the challenge is we're nearly almost all scatterbrained. So even as we go from one last thing to one last thing, our productivity is way down.

I've measured this for myself. From 8:00 p.m. to 10:00 p.m., it takes me two to three times as long to get things done as earlier in the day.

And then after 10:00 it's five to ten times as long, as I barely grind away and get pulled off track, and off track, and off—well, you get the idea.

Getting to bed earlier has profound effects on your health, body, mind, and soul. Like any other animal, we were meant to be in sync with the earth. We have a circadian rhythm in our body that causes systems to rise and fall in sync with the sun.

The trick is that we don't want to make radical changes all at once. I'm what I call the "kind-gentle-easy-good" guy. I like to make tiny changes over massive periods of time, rather than massive changes over tiny periods of time. Why? Because tiny, kind, and gentle changes stick, creating permanent habits, while massive radical changes hurt, and we boomerang back.

So when it comes to shifting your bedtime, I recommend shifting the time you go to sleep, or rolling it back, fifteen minutes earlier, every two to three days. And you can do the same for the time you get up as well.

Now it's true, as any great meditator will tell you, when you meditate first thing in the morning, you won't need quite as much sleep. So don't worry about getting up just a little bit earlier. The fact that it calms you and detunes your nervous system means you'll use less frenetic energy throughout the day, and you'll feel more rested and refreshed, even with a tiny bit less sleep. Put another way, even though you may be getting fewer hours of sleep, you actually feel more rested throughout the day because AWE has put you in a calmer, more relaxed state.

Again, the key here is tiny. I don't want you to go from waking at 7:00 or 8:00, or even 10:00 to suddenly getting up at 5:00. That'll hurt badly, and soon enough you'll think your willpower's not strong enough, and you'll give up. But your willpower isn't weak. With a radical shift, you've just induced jet lag, and now are being told you have to write on top of that. That just won't work. To learn a better way to start your day, check out our program at www.MagicalRoutine.com.

Recruit Assistance

One of the keys to success with automatic writing is to have your family onboard. If they want you to stay up late, or get up with you first thing in the morning, that's a challenge. So ask your family if they can help you out, either going to bed at the same time you do, or allowing you to dim the lights and make your evening more like time at a local campground—they may actually like the dimmed lights or candlelight.

Alert your family to your new plan so they can be supportive. This may also mean no heavy conversations at night. Come up with a family plan that helps you get to bed earlier. This isn't just good for you, it's good for everyone.

Now what about if your "thing" to do with your partner is to watch a late night crime show or favorite zombie thriller. Well, going back to what I said earlier, that's probably not how you want to reprogram the mind, but what about shutting off the electronics and hopping into bed to actually talk with each other or snuggle or enjoy swapping massages. These can be ten times more fun, great bonding experiences, and get you to bed ten times earlier.

No matter what you do, or who you recruit, get the electronics off, the lights dim, and step away from Facebook and email and leftovers in the fridge—all the activities that don't serve you—and get to bed.

Hot lavender-infused or Epson salt bath before bed anyone? Make your evening time sacred and as relaxing as you can.

Ask in AWE

When you're really struggling with something, I always say bring it to AWE. If you've been able to connect with that higher wisdom or your guides, then ask for help. *How do I get to bed earlier? What systems do*

I put into place? Or even, *Why am I stuck, no matter how much I try, I can't seem to get myself to bed earlier?*

Ask for help and see what you hear. For myself, my guides been instrumental both for my bedtime and getting up earlier. In fact, they're incessantly challenging me to get up even earlier, as they say they have more and more to teach.

Tibetan Monk Bedtime Ritual

If you're feeling stressed, overwhelmed, or feel as if you just didn't get anything done during the day, and you're now upset or a smoldering ruin, then this technique can help.

Some people use the Benjamin Franklin technique and write out or revisit their to-dos before bedtime. DANGER: While this exercise does help you get your schedule settled for the following day, if you have a fragile ego that's just looking for reasons to clobber you—as mine used to—then this technique will simply point out your supposed inadequacies or why you failed today. Why? Because in the history of mankind, no one has ever finished their to-do list. Not once, not ever. Why? Because you can always find something to add, which means making a list and checking it twice can leave you feeling hollow and inadequate at best.

That's why I teach people a bedtime daily review that was used by ancient Tibetan monks. In essence you're going to review your day in reverse, from the most recent events (such as doing this exercise) to your earliest, waking and rising. By doing this you build temporal space between you and what took place. What's temporal space? It means that we can warp time, based on how we view things and how much "space" we put between ourselves and another activity.

A perfect example of this is taking a trip, or even an airplane flight. Let's say you get up early, go to the airport, and fly to Europe, or even simply from New York to LA. Even though you start and finish the trip on the same day, because of the distance involved, it will feel like days or weeks ago since you left. That's actually why Jessica and I often travel by RV because distance helps build space, sometimes especially important for new ideas, new beginnings, or healing.

We can build this same "distance" by reviewing our day in reverse. How to begin?

Let's say it's 10:00 p.m., you're going to bed, and you are worried about a meeting you had with your boss or something your daughter said or an aging parent who has needs. You write down, "Nine o'clock, what was I doing? I was cleaning. Eight o'clock, I was checking email and there was something disturbing there. Seven o'clock, I know I'm supposed to eat earlier but that's when I actually finished dinner. Six o'clock was cooking dinner. Five o'clock, I had been to the gym after work," and you roll back your day. Hour by hour.

What happens is by the time you write out your day, you have built temporal space between you and your most recent worries and concerns. They seem an entire day away. You have just wiped the slate clean. Now you can go to bed and those worries and concerns seem like such a distant event that they're not on your mind. The last thing you can do if your mind is still worried: go to prayer, go to surrender, or simply go to a mantra.

Sync with the Sun

For those living at latitudes where it's dark, dreary, and cold in the winter, and the thought alone of walking outside would turn you into a Popsicle, I highly recommend a SAD lamp (seasonal affective disorder or SAD is a form of depression that can be remedied if you sit in artificial sunlight for a period of time indoors).

With that said, whenever I work with a coaching client who struggles with their attention, or their ability to sleep, I give them a challenge—and I'm going to give the same to you. See if you can go for a walk at either sunrise or sunset. This helps sync your internal clock we mentioned earlier to the natural cycle of the planet.

If you can't get out for a walk, at least get outside at sunrise for just five or ten minutes. For myself, with a busy summer schedule, I take walks outside at sunset and sit with the sun at sunrise. Okay, technically, I have chipmunks and squirrels in my lap at sunrise depending on where I am—a tale for another day—but that syncing up with the sun is incredibly powerful. I feel more relaxed throughout the day, and the practice gives me the greatest night's sleep—and more energy. That alone makes a massive difference for me.

I'm what I call a gazer. And I'll share just a bit about it, but I am not recommending it for you, but it's what works for me.

Living in the mountains, it takes a little while for that sun to get up above the mountains, but every single day without fail, I am watching for that sun to come up. For that first thirty seconds that it's up until it's really popped up above the mountains, I'm making that connection, which is resetting my optic nerve and resetting my melatonin production. To me, it feels like there's healing energy in watching the sun at sunrise and sunset. And I'm told, backed by science, the red light at sunrise and sunset does some phenomenal things for our bodies.

I really started doing this gazing after my second near-death experience and started calling my gazing at the sunrise my vitamin time, as I felt as if I was getting a healthy healing dose of vitamins each time I'd sit. If you find this topic interesting, check out my interview with Linda Geddes, author of *Chasing the Sun* at www.InspireNationShow.com.

On winter days when the sun is not out I'm doing the same thing artificially with my SAD lamp.

I'm going to give you the nontechnical version of why this works because I am not a scientist. A SAD lamp basically beams you with a very bright white light. It's a full spectrum light, which means it is basically all the colors that you would get out of sunlight.

Desk or floor lamps come in either 5,000 lux or 10,000 lux. Maybe they're even more brilliant than that, but 10,000 seems to be the standard. My SAD lamp looks like a series of LED lights. When we lived on the East Coast of the US, I would eat breakfast with the lamp close by blasting my face for ten to twenty minutes.

This lamp, like the sun, resets your optic nerve and your melatonin production, and it gives you a massive boost of energy. However, it won't help your body produce vitamin D, an essential vitamin you get from the sun (or supplements of D3). What a SAD lamp will do is affect all of your hormones normally affected by sunlight.

This is not medical advice. Please seek medical advice from your doctor. For the purposes of improving your sleep, here is what I suggest: Use your SAD lamp ten to twenty minutes twice a day. First, use it around sunrise. In the middle of the winter, especially if you live at a latitude closer to the North and South Poles, start beaming yourself even before sunrise. For your second session, turn on the lamp midafternoon about 3:00 or 4:00 p.m. when your energy is waning and you're wondering how you are going to make it through the rest of the workday.

That light will give you a burst and a boost of energy to help carry you forward.

A final note about when to experience automatic writing. There are no rules in life. There are no rules with AWE, there's no judgment. If you're a night owl, let's take advantage of it. Just make sure, if possible, your house is sleeping and the environment around you is quiet. When the rest of the world sleeps on either end is when you're going to get those deepest words.

During my thirty years of coaching, I've learned to look at sleep. Starting with athletes, then students and adults with attention deficit disorder, I discovered that many of their problems and challenges stemmed from a lack of good sleep. Once my coaching clients started sleeping better, they experienced greater focus, greater concentration, and felt less overwhelmed, depressed, and anxious—something that everyone can benefit from.

I have an entire program dedicated to help you get a better night's sleep called the Magical Evening Routine. You can find it at www .MagicalEveningRoutine.com.

5 | How Automatic Writing Steered Me Back on Track

J essica and I started our *Inspire Nation* show because of our automatic writing experience. We envisioned the concept, the structure, and the rebuilding of our lives—and health—after we found ourselves living our darkest days—you could say the dark night of our souls.

Flash back to a remote, chilly creek bed just outside Lake Tahoe. I was dying. The medical helicopter was on the way. When paramedics arrived, they found no blood pressure.

Jessica and I had been on a book tour with our *Barefoot Running* book throughout forty-three states. By 2011 we were living on Maui, had lectured in Southeast Asia, and had completed our second book together, *Barefoot Walking*, which to me is like a walking meditation.

We found ourselves in an unreliable RV on another book tour for the walking version. At that point, we had been working our tails off, yet something felt wrong. Sure we had publisher challenges and didn't feel supported. But something was off, way off, so we were returning the mechanically unsound RV and headed home to Maui.

I was not supposed to be pushing this way on the tour. Exhausted. Discouraged. We stayed one more night at Lake Tahoe. The next morning we were to head out to return the RV, just four hours away, when we saw a trailhead off the road called Pyramid Creek Trail, which leads to Horsetail Falls. We decided on one last hike in the Sierras to clear our heads.

At the end of the trail was a freezing-cold mountain water hole, carved in granite from snowy ice-melt from a cornice up above. As I love cold-water dips, the temptation was too much. After three dips below the surface to a mini underwater cave (there was a blissful silence just feet beneath the surface in this frigid pristine paradise), I was turning blue, and it was time to get dressed, warm up, and head back to the RV.

For the return trip, I put on my leather-soled moccasins. In my exhilaration, I hugged Jessica and told her I was ready to have children with her. It was a profound revelation for us. We headed home.

She crossed at the narrowest creek flow, and as I followed, it happened. I stepped in the creek, then out and onto a slippery rock, and went flying through the air. I landed on a pyramid-shaped rock right on my thigh. It was like an artillery shell went off and exploded my femur. I yelled, "Oh, no. Not again!"

Not again referred to an inline skating accident in 2006 when I deliberately threw myself up and backward to avoid a baby whose father was inadvertently out on a bike path, while teaching his baby how to walk. At that time, I was sponsored by Rollerblade and training for a 4,000-mile, forty-day record skate across the country to help those with learning challenges (similar to a cross-country solo bike ride I did a few years earlier to bring attention to people with attention deficit disorder and other similar challenges).

In that first incident, avoiding hitting the baby, in a moment of grace and necessity, I found myself lying next to the trail (toddler was safe) with a shattered hip, femur, and arm, and later I was lying in the hospital with a brand new titanium femur and hip, plus an inch-long leg length disparity. Rehabbing back from that accident took years.

So in the freezing creek bed, some seven years, one month, and seventeen days later, I felt shards of my right femur nearly piercing through the skin (as I was slowly bleeding to death internally).

That first near-death experience started me down this process of the open-hearted warrior because, in that moment, I experienced a feeling of joy, of bliss, of love, of fulfillment, of life is good. This is where my WOO HOO started. I had never WOO HOO-ed a day in my life before that.

Thinking they were dealing with a lunatic with a head injury who was WOO HOO-ing to breathe, the emergency workers kept asking one question, "Did you hit your head?" I hadn't hit my head; my helmet was intact. I felt so much love and joy and happiness and oneness and understanding of the world that I didn't have before this near-death experience. I knew this would be a completely different path and a different trajectory. To me, I had just won the lottery.

So, too, I knew that I was experiencing the most horrendous pain and spasms I had ever felt in my life with what turned out to be a mirror injury on my other hip. In an instant, I had stopped breathing and was given a choice. I had been given a choice to let go, fall into bliss, and leave this world, or to fight, experience perhaps the most intense pain I ever had—plus at least another year of grizzly rehab and to force my way back.

Having just told Jessica I was ready to have kids with her, there was no letting go. So I had to force myself to breathe for the next hour, until the emergency crews got to our remote location and struggled to stabilize me before loading me into the first of two helicopters that transported me to Barton Memorial where an ace orthopedic surgeon near the ski resort was called upon to put Humpty Dumpty back together once again.

The day after the surgery the physician's assistant (PA) who aided with the procedure came in and asked how in the world I'd gotten the X-rays up on my website so fast. I told him I had no idea what he meant.

Turns out the injuries were identical—with matching twin titanium femurs, titanium hips, and even the metal wire loops that held everything together—and no more leg length discrepancy, I was now even.

The doc in Tahoe said, "The odds of having one accident like this are one in a million. The odds of having the same accident twice? One in infinity." To me, this was Universe speaking loud and clear, "Everything happens for a reason, and I'm going to give you the most dramatic example of it possible. Every step for the rest of your life, you'll remember. Everything happens for a reason."

I faced another long road of rehabilitation in California and eventually back home on Maui.

Perhaps I should have seen this coming.

By the age of two, I had three sets of stitches in my head. I was a whirlwind of activity in a crazy household. I was first diagnosed at the age of five with hyperactivity, now called ADHD.

My medicine of choice, after I was taken off Ritalin, was riding my bicycle around the block and around and around and around. There's an irony that at age ten I ended up in a street drag race against the babysitter's cousin on my little Huffy 56 Thunder. Flying down the road neck and neck, she hit a rock, hit my front wheel, and I went soaring. I broke my femur, kneecap, and tibia, and I had a cast from my foot all the way up to my hip.

That "little" accident was one of the best things that ever happened to me because, after six operations over a period of two years with time in a wheelchair and crutches in between, I learned compassion, kindness, and understanding.

But, most importantly, I learned that everything we're told about what's real and what's not is wrong, and that we are more in charge of our bodies than we could ever imagine.

After that bike calamity, the doctor said, "You're going to be lucky to walk again. By eighteen, you're going to have severe arthritis. You're never going to be able to be active."

I went on to become a professional cyclist.

By eighteen, I went to Colorado College because I wanted to race bicycles in Europe, and I wanted to train in the mountains and at the velodrome in Colorado Springs. I trained often at the Olympic Training Center for cycling and speed skating and for the collegiate national cycling championships.

I got myself to race in Europe and would alternate between half a year racing in Europe, and studying and training in Colorado Springs. I even ran the Rocky Mountain Collegiate Cycling Conference for a year.

In between I was hit head-on by a motorcyclist on a bicycle trail after coming back from Europe. I can still recall what he said as he lifted his 700cc motorcycle off me: "I killed him, I can't believe I killed him." Au contraire, but the accidents continued.

I was racing for a French team outside of the extravagant mountain getaway town of Annecy, when I was invited to a very special road race through the high Alps. It was there, in the town of Hauteville, where the biggie happened.

I was coming through a blind uphill turn with crowds cheering on l'Américain. A safety official had just waved me though the turn, inadvertently right into an oncoming car. An elderly woman had come up an alley and gotten her full-sized Peugeot out onto the course. I managed to get myself sideways before she hit me.

I flew through the air, and when I landed I thought, "I'm okay, I'm okay." Then I looked down and saw my left leg with a 90 degree bend in it. It was like a scene out of the Stephen King's novel *Misery*, where the hero's leg is hit with a sledgehammer and knocked sideways—called a hobbling.

In an instant I went from thinking "Life is good," to thinking, "I'll never race again, my dream is dead, God is dead, there is no God." I was in such pain I had to force myself to keep from biting the pavement, instead clawing the pavement with my fingers with such force it took weeks for the asphalt to come out from under my nails. In the hospital they "cold set" my leg (read 8 people tugging at my leg to snap it back in place, *without* anesthetic) and it was 16 ours in "observation" screaming and wailing, before they'd give me pain killers. Had I had a gun, I may have taken my life for the pain I was in.

Someone once said your body keeps the score. Your body is a reflection of what's going on internally. I didn't have a means of addressing the wounds from the traumas that took place.

The titanium rod soon inserted through my lower leg was temporary, but the PTSD wasn't so temporary. I struggled for the next seven years with how the trauma was reflected in my body.

Fast-forward through this time, I experienced something called The Native American Church. I had a girlfriend for six and a half years who was Navajo. There I was in a sweat lodge, feet on the earth. From sundown to sunrise. There's a medicine man with the coals. Somebody is drumming.

That was the first time that I really experienced anything greater than myself. I truly felt I was not alone. That ceremony set the stage for later on. By 2004, I had a couple masters degrees at this point, an

MBA and a master's in computers. I had been coaching people, first in athletics and then life coaching for nearly fifteen years.

I had also been meditating for over a decade. I had learned to quiet and calm my mind, and I challenged anybody who said "ADHD is for life." Not a chance. You can use the gifts of a hyper-creative mind. You can turn it on when you want; you can turn it off when you want.

I found a new level of quiet, of silence, and of feeling not alone. And the voice of automatic writing was starting to come up in those quieter moments.

After my first near-death accident with the baby on the path, I struggled with overuse injuries while trying to walk and run again, until I heard in meditation, *you tried everything else, why not try going barefoot.* I thought, "Me? Mr. Flatfoot, Mr. Plantar Fasciitis go barefoot?" But I listened, and gave it a try. My feet grew stronger and stronger, and I healed. And my mind began to go quiet the more I touched to the earth.

I was plugging in and that's when Jessica came along. I met her at a Buddhist meditation center after I heard the voice of AWE again in meditation. I was told it was time to get out of the woods. Time to go find community, and there I was likely to meet someone, the girl in my dreams, quite literally.

And then, only a month later, there she was.

Months later, Jessica started a barefoot running club. One day she announced, "You're teaching tomorrow." I had no idea, but there were ten people there, then ten more, and the next thing you know, we had a club of over a hundred, and she announced, "You're writing a book." And it became the best-seller *Barefoot Running.*

On and on it went. When I was running barefoot connected to the earth and quieting the mind, I truly began to hear that wise, still voice of AWE. At the time barefoot running was that bridge.

The AWE-some Experience Is Born

Two near-death experiences later and two titanium hips later—we were living on Maui, yet feeling lost. For anywhere from one to four hours a day, each and every day, I was meditating and diving into silence. I even held space at a meditation center for hours each day. Yet I wasn't getting direction in life. And I was struggling to make a full comeback from my injuries.

I was introduced to Richard Yiap, an amazing healer. He had this incredible technology and actually hooked me up to something like jumper cables and had me do breathing exercises. The machine was showing me all of my Chinese pulses. It measured my biological age of a forty-year-old, but said my health age was more like eighty or ninety because of my fragile health.

His partner, Sian Chua, was teaching a course on accessing the Akashic records and being able to hear from the Akashic Masters, kind of like the librarians of life or the librarians of the Universe. It sounded like an amazing opportunity, so both Jessica and I signed up.

At the end of the course, we were learning how to write to and from the Akashic Masters. I got the most profound words of wisdom, similar to diving into AWE. Then I had to repeat them back to the class. Out. Loud. That's where the trouble began.

The automatic writing was about how great I was—really about how great all of us are—but my ego would not accept this. My writing talked about how I would be a world change maker. And how I would speak as if from a mountain top to millions below.

At the time, I thought this was ego. That this was completely made up. This was bogus. That I was completely trying to show off to the entire class, and that this was complete and total—well, you get the idea.

That was truly my first time with an automatic writing experience. I had no idea how profound and powerful the words would be or how they would demand me to be so much greater than I was at the time.

I felt so unsure where to go with this message, or if it even had a thread of truth, that I wouldn't touch it for a few years. However, a couple years later, Sian met with me and brought me through a past-life regression. She had been trained by renowned hypnotist Dolores Cannon in this technique. In the process, I was given more words of grandeur that drove me just as nuts. I still wouldn't believe it and wouldn't touch the message or automatic writing for nearly another year.

When I finally tried automatic writing again, I still wouldn't believe what was coming up. My ego was telling me I had made up all this grandeur about speaking to multitudes. I can remember being on the beach in Maui walking with Jessica and saying there must be some meaning behind this.

On the challenging news side, because I was still rehabbing, I wasn't working. We were struggling to put out a video-based learning program on mindful running (www.MindfulRunning.org). We were facing financial ruin, and then Jessica's health fell apart.

Of course, later we discovered her health and our finances failing was a huge gift. And I finally began to dive into automatic writing. Desperation is a powerful elixir for change.

I needed some way to tap into Spirit and figure out what in the world was going on. I turned to automatic writing to figure out why we were stuck, why things appeared to be going so wrong, and what to do to get out of this mess. I was brave enough and bold enough to take what Sian taught us and to modify and change it. I was feeling an intuitive process about what felt right for us, and a rudimentary form of AWE was birthed.

We ended up leaving Maui, broke but not broken, and moved back to New Jersey to live with Jessica's family, leaving everything behind except for our kitty cats. We moved into her childhood bedroom with two twin mattresses on the floor.

As much as it wasn't an ideal living situation, everything good came out of being in New Jersey. Yet it happened so fast. Our heads were spinning. I never got to say goodbye to our home on Maui. I never got to say goodbye to our land that we were on. Instead I was whisking everything into storage, my head spinning, trying to get the house ready.

And there we found it: an inch-thick carpet of mold in the rafters, which is what had gotten Jessica sick. Once we found it, we knew how to heal—and AWE helped us with that as well.

In New Jersey, automatic writing became my oxygen. Our *Inspire Nation* show was conceived. We rebounded our health and our finances. We moved out of her childhood bedroom. We found a haven back in Colorado in the Rockies. And that ego thing about speaking from a mountain top to millions? Well? The Universe was right. Our studio was literally on a hill overlooking the valley and town below, where I spoke before millions. I just didn't see it at the time.

6 | A Brief History of Automatic Writing

I must admit I'm not a student of history, and while some spiritual concepts and practices come from a lineage or a great master, the automatic writing I teach in this book is not based on age-old techniques honed over thousands of years—though automatic writing has existed in one form or another for at least that long.

The process of automatic writing is not new, however. And as much as I'd like to take some credit for its origins, I cannot. I have just modified the experience, as I explained in the last chapter, as part of my recovery story in my own practice.

Here is what I do know about the automatic writing experience I call AWE. The practice has likely been around for as long as there has been writing. I've found automatic writing used in the Bible, in ancient spiritual texts, in early psychology, in modern psychology, and in more contemporary books categorized as spirituality and healing.

Automatic writing has existed through the ages, whether called channeled writing, intuitive writing, psychography, automatism, surrealist writing, scrying, or even spirit writing. The practice has existed for thousands of years, perhaps since the time of Homer and the *Iliad*, and certainly since the Hebrew Bible and the Koran. Wherever it's said that God spoke, and the word were transcribed, one finds automatic writing. It can certainly be found in other religious texts, and even in ancient Chinese writing called spirit writing.

Countless writers over the ages have simply put pen to paper (or even charcoal, feathers, or sticks dipped in ink) and found the words flowing. Let us imagine a time when humans first took a feather and drew it to ink, or even took a stone to chisel granite—words have been flowing.

According to Encyclopedia.com, "Parts of the Jewish Bible (the Christian Old Testament) were received through automatic writing, for example 2 Chronicles 21:12 says, 'And there came a writing to him from Elijah the prophet saying . . .'"

And in the West, in modern history there's no end to the number of people, including influential scientists who have used, studied, or written about automatic writing. One early instance is the scientist Emmanuel Swedenborg (1688–1772) who used a process of automatism or automatic writing, well before there was such a term. Describing his writing, he said, "There have sometimes been sent to me papers covered in writing; some of which are exactly like papers written by hand, and others like papers that had been printed in the world."

Automatic writing's popularity took off in the mid-1800s during the spiritualism movement, which lasted into the early 1900s in the US, based on the belief that departed souls can interact with the living. It grew even further in the UK, having a substantial revival in the 1950s after the repeal of witchcraft laws and has been most popular in France and Brazil. Here in the US, it has had a rebirth in popularity as the New Age movement began (my source is *Britannica*).

During the early heyday of spiritualism, people were looking for a faster way to communicate with spirits and tried many techniques including using a planchette, or a "spirit guided" device that held a pen. It was essentially a board with a pencil or pen designed to take the user's thinking mind out of the process and help them connect with Spirit. This planchette was later replaced with direct writing, with the user finding they didn't need the planchette. And thus, automatic writing was popularized. I see some parallels here to a Ouija board.

In 1930 psychologist Anita M. Muhl wrote a book titled *Automatic Writing: An Approach to the Unconscious*. She shares that automatic writing (at the time) had had its heyday in the mid to late 1800s as a powerful clinical psychological technique for working with the subconscious. And she was working to bring the technique back. Here I am, nearly a hundred years later, unknowingly (until now), continuing her work.

Spirit Writing (I Write Dead People)

What's most fascinating is that similar devices to the planchettes, called phoenix baskets, were used by the Chinese back to the time of Confucianism, Daoism, and before (and still in use today in some sects of Daoism). This has been called spirit writing or Fuji writing. Entire religions in the Far East were based on this channeling, where a scrawling device was inserted or held by wood and guided by one hand to carve or scrawl Chinese characters onto paper or onto sand.

A few notable authors during the spiritualist movement (as cited from the *New World Encyclopedia*) include these spiritualists:

Pearl Curran, a St. Louis housewife, began to communicate with a spirit named Patience Worth who was said to be an Englishwoman from Dorsetshire, England, in either 1649 or 1694, who said she came to America where she was murdered by Native Americans. All told, Curran is said to have written over 400,000 words including nearly 5,000 poems, several novels, a play, and many shorter pieces.

What's most fascinating to me is that experts who read Curran's work said it was accurate for the time period (1600s) and that there was no way she could have replicated it. According to the American Hauntings account of "The Mystery of Patience Worth" (and confirmed by the summary in *New World Encyclopedia*), no one ever verified that Patience Worth actually lived in the 1600s, and experts who studied Curran's writing doubted that she could have produced the works attributed to the ghost on her own (unlikely that Pearl Curran would have been able to create the literary style, vocabulary, history, or subject matter) because Curran had a limited education, no knowledge of the language used during that earlier time period, and was unaware of the history of the time. Experts speculated that the writing was of Curran's spiritual counterpart.

Hélène Smith, born in 1861, was a well-known Swiss medium who went by the fictitious name of Catherine Elise Muller. Surrealists dubbed her the "Muse of Automatic Writing." According to historians, "In addition to claims of past lives as a Hindu princess and Marie Antoinette, Smith produced automatic writing in Arabic and what she claimed were the languages of Mars and Uranus, which she then translated into French."

Francisco Chico Xavier, a medium from Brazil, born in 1910, was said to have written hundreds of thousands of pages in automatic writing. He began in primary school, where he even won a literary essay contest that he said came from Spirit. While he never continued his education, he continued his writing, including many books, and it's said his scientific and literary quality were far beyond his possible abilities.

Another famous spiritualist who used automatic writing was **William Stainton Moses,** who went on to help found the Society for Psychical Research. He was originally a highly educated ordained minister who found himself drawn to automatic writing after investigating seances. He is best known for his books *Spirit Teachings* (1883) and *Spirit Identity* (1879), which were written through automatic writing.

I don't claim that AWE will turn you into a carnival sideshow with literary acumen. But I do find that accounts of spiritualists and others in history to be a fascinating sidebar to our discussion of automatic writing and its evolution through the ages.

Automatic Writing as Therapy and through Art

Automatic writing has also been used for nearly 150 years as a form of therapy. It's been a powerful way for people to get out of their thinking minds (as I have been explaining the process) and to be used as a tool to study and rewire the subconscious.

It's been used by Freudian psychologists, including **Carl Jung,** who is said to have written *Seven Sermons to the Dead* through automatic writing just weeks after breaking with Sigmund Freud.

William James (1842–1910) was an American psychologist who taught the first course on psychology in the US. It was during a time in which science and spiritualism were not nearly as far apart as they are today. He was also the first researcher in parapsychology or PSI and was fascinated with automatic writing and channeling.

From his paper "Notes on Automatic Writing," James discussed whether a person is fully conscious of pain and pressure while writing, or what he called an anesthesia effect while doing automatic writing.

He wrote: "I have actually tested three automatic writers for anaesthesia. In one of them, examined between the acts of writing, no anaesthesia was observed, but the examination was superficial. In the two others, both of them men, the anaesthesia to pricking and pinching, and possibly to touch, seemed complete."

Sidney Dean was a Connecticut Republican congressman from 1857 to 1859. In a letter to Professor William James of Harvard, the congressman claimed he wrote with apparently two different minds and produced symbols and foreign languages.

Dean wrote: "The writing is in my own hand, but the dictation not of my own mind and will, but that of another, upon subjects of which I can have no knowledge and hardly a theory; and I, myself, consciously criticize the thought, fact, mode of expressing it, etc., while the hand is recording the subject-matter and even the words impressed to be written. If I refuse to write the sentence, or even the word, the impression instantly ceases, and my willingness must be mentally expressed before the work is resumed, and it is resumed at the point of cessation, even if it should be in the middle of a sentence. Sentences are commenced without knowledge of mine as to their subject or ending. In fact, I have never known in advance the subject of disquisition."

From the world of psychology to art, the early influence of automatic writing was evident as I dug deeper for history. Surrealism was a movement in the 1920s against the "rationalism" in the past, or in simpler terms, a pushback against just blindly following the rational mind—and in modern terms, I'd say tapping into intuition or perhaps even into the heart.

One of the most famous surrealists to use automatic writing was the cofounder of the surrealism movement, **Andre Breton**, known as "The Father of Surrealism." He published *The Surrealist Manifesto* in 1924 in which I found this description: "Surrealism was a means of reuniting conscious and unconscious realms of experience so completely that the world of dream and fantasy would be joined to the everyday rational world in 'an absolute reality, a surreality.'"

According to surrealists and Breton, it's tapping into the subconscious and imagination that equated true genius, and he saw automatic writing as one such vehicle.

Along with the French writer, **Philippe Soupault** (1897–1990), Breton wrote the first surrealist work, an example of automatic writing, in a novel called *Les Champs Magnétiques* (translated as The Magnetic Fields). There are countless examples of surrealist writers using automatic writing.

And then there's automatic drawing, a topic more for another book, which includes the likes of such surrealist and artistic giants as **Salvador Dali,** known to paint in a hypnagogic state.

Moving beyond surrealism, many more traditional poets and authors are said to have devised at least a portion of their work through automatic writing. Literary giant **William Blake** is not the only famous poet who admits to having dabbled in automatic writing (I say admits, because how many poets have not had poems flow to them from "inspiration."). And while it is not known whether poet William Butler Yeats (1865–1939) used automatic writing for his poetry, his wife Georgiana Hyde-Lees is known to have written through automatic writing.

It's said that the medium **Thomas Lake Harris**, famous in the nineteenth century, produced a significant amount of poetry through automatic writing as well. And other famous people of the nineteenth century who produced works from automatic writing are Goethe, Victor Hugo, and Victorien Sardou.

One of the most powerful, and unusual, descriptions of automatic writing from that century I've read is from **Stainton Moses** who wrote in *Spirit Identity* (1879): "My right arm was seized about the middle of the forearm, and dashed violently up and down with a noise resembling that of a number of paviors [ramming down concrete block] at work. It was the most tremendous exhibition of 'unconscious muscular action' I ever saw. In vain I tried to stop it. I distinctly felt the grasps, soft and firm, round my arm, and though perfectly possessed of senses and volition, I was powerless to interfere, although my hand was disabled for some days by the bruising it then got."

While this is fascinating, no one I know has been seized, bruised, or forced (far from it) to write.

The focus of automatic writing changed. Outside of psychology, while many nineteenth-century writers focused their automatic writing on communicating with the dead, by the time of the New Age movement in the twentieth century, communication was focused on Spirit in general, not just the dead, and by whatever means it would arrive. Many famous authors felt they dictated their work, which may or may not be technically considered automatic writing.

These include **Helen Schucman** who channeled *A Course in Miracles*, **Jane Roberts**, who wrote the *Seth Material,* and even **Neale Donald Walsch**, whom I spoke with personally about this, who says he heard a voice and dictated the *Conversations with God* series rather than it being automatic writing. He would say it was dictation, not automatic writing, so it is hard to say. Is dictation an extension of automatic writing? I hear the voice of AWE throughout the day, so it's hard to say where AWE begins and where it ends. You'll have to judge for yourself.

From Dickens to Baker Street to Red Hot Chili Peppers

In addition to older religious texts such as the Bible and Koran potentially being written, at least partially, in automatic writing, in 1882, a dentist brought us one more. **John Ballou Newbrough**, a British American dentist wrote *Oahspe: A New Bible* through automatic writing. It was a version of the Bible that contained what he called "new revelations" and was written by "the Embassadors of the angel hosts of heaven prepared and revealed unto man in the name of Jehovih."

The famous novelist **Charles Dickens** passed away in 1870 before he could finish his last novel, *The Mystery of Edwin Drood*. But then enter **Thomas Power James**, better known as TP James, a book publisher in Brattleboro, Vermont. According to James, Charles Dickens came through to him in automatic writing, and he wrote the rest of the Dickens novel. James went on to publish the novel in 1873 under the title *Part Second of the Mystery of Edwin Drood*.

Sir Arthur Conan Doyle, the famed author of the Sherlock Holmes stories, was a known spiritualist and automatic writer. He even wrote about it in *The New Revelation* (1918). More interestingly, his wife invited Houdini to a seance where she wrote fifteen pages in automatic writing apparently from Houdini's mother during a session.

I've had countless clients come up with poetry and lyrics in their automatic writing, and I share some in chapter 8, so it's no surprise that professional artists have done the same. At the top of the list is **David Byrne** who discussed his use of automatic writing with *GQ* magazine. Oddly enough he's even been influenced by fellow poet and automatic writer **William Blake** in albums such as *Utopia*.

Van Morrison is another musician who admits to using automatic writing for his work. In the *New Yorker* he shared how he used it for his album *Astral Weeks*. And then, most interesting to me, is an experimental band made up of several members of the **Red Hot Chili Peppers** that titled their first album *Automatic Writing* and their second *AW 2*.

It's fascinating to me how long automatic writing has been around, how it's been used by psychologists and sages alike, and by musicians, artists, and authors, and yet how little the practice is known and used by the general public.

My goal is to ride on the shoulders of giants, whether I knew I was or not, and bring this age-old, yet newer than ever technique, out to everyone, everywhere, so we can all tap into AWE. Can you imagine how much better the world would be if we were all tapped into our inner guidance or something greater than ourselves?

7 | And the Science Says . . .

Do you know that your brain literally changes during the process of automatic writing? Though I am not a neuro-scientist per se, I love to geek out on it, and have had many of the world's top brain scientists on the show. So I asked them to explain the process. I summarize their work for you in this chapter.

We know the brain changes because we can see the changes. Here's how. One of the coolest tools in science is the single photon emission computed tomography device, affectionately known as a SPECT scan (like the familiar CT scan you already know about). And to me, the reason this imaging is so cool is that you can look into the brain and see what's happening when someone's doing automatic writing.

Technically, you can see what areas of the brain light up during AWE, which parts of the brain power down, and even long-term changes to the brain.

Admittedly, more research needs to be done in this area, but Andrew Newberg, MD, is pioneering the field of studying spirituality and the brain. He's my hero.

In 2012 he published a study of ten automatic writing practitioners, also known as Brazilian psychographers (his description). Five of these practitioners had extensive automatic writing experience, and five were called "less expert mediums." His results were fascinating. I have included a link to the peer-reviewed scientific article for your science geek friends (see Resources).

To summarize Dr. Newberg's study, in experienced automatic writing practitioners, their brains literally change during the process when viewed by SPECT scans of their frontal lobes (the parts of the brain responsible for thinking and writing).

Dr. Newberg told me: "So basically, what we found was that for people who are highly experienced [in automatic writing] there was essentially a decrease of activity in a number of brain regions, including areas involved in language, like the temporal lobe and parts of the frontal lobe."

For those who want to skip the science part, if you read just one sentence in this chapter, this is it: **In essence, studies show that the experienced practitioners of automatic writing are not using their thinking minds to come up with the words that are coming out on paper.**

Now for the rest of us who want to dig into the geeky science, I present my experts: Andrew Newberg, MD, is Research Director at the Marcus Institute of Integrative Health at Thomas Jefferson University in Philadelphia. And Dean Radin, PhD, cited later, is Chief Scientist at the Institute for Noetic Sciences and a leading researcher on parapsychology. Both have been guests on my *Inspire Nation* show, and I invite you to listen to their interviews archived on our website at www.InspireNationShow.com.

This Is Your Brain on Automatic Writing

Certain parts of your brain are expected to light up during the act of writing—everyday writing, that is. By light up, I mean blood flow is measured during the scans. Now what's really fascinating is that these areas of the brain that you'd expect to light up during writing actually power down during automatic writing. Your temporal lobe is one of them.

Your temporal lobe and parts of your frontal lobe are the parts of the brain responsible for language. According to Dr. Newberg, "[The temporal lobe is] involved in how we process language or think about language or reflect on language." He goes on to say we might expect it to light up during writing, but in experienced channelers, it's the direct opposite; there is instead a decrease in blood flow to the temporal lobe."

Why do the frontal and temporal lobes power down for automatic writing? While there's no scientific explanation yet, my guess is that it's because the language isn't coming from us, it's being channeled either from inside or outside of ourselves, but not from the thinking mind.

Your hippocampus is involved in conscious memory. So one would expect when you're journaling, or writing from memory, this area would light up. However, just like with the frontal lobe and temporal lobe, again, in the experienced group of automatic writers in Dr. Newberg's study, it was less.

What could this mean? That your automatic writing is not drawing from working memory in your brain. Instead, the words are coming from somewhere else. Which makes perfect sense, because journaling is drawing from your conscious memory, while AWE is tapping into something else.

I recently interviewed Kyle Gray, author of eight books on angels and the creator of four oracle decks to communicate with angels. We were talking about clairsentience, or feeling messages from the Universe. And in many ways, that may be what's going on in AWE. I'm extrapolating from the data a bit, but it appears that the messages coming to the psychographers in Dr. Newberg's study may be coming through the emotional centers of the brain, rather than from the verbal or word-generating sections of the brain.

One thing that I found fascinating has to do with areas of the brain called the precentral gyrus and another called the anterior cortex. These are both involved in attentional processes and regulating various cognitive processes. In essence when you're focused, and paying attention, you'd expect these areas to light up.

And that's just what they did in the beginners to automatic writing who were trying to "focus" to write. These areas lit up. However, in the experienced automatic writing practitioners who have learned to defuse their focus, or let go of focusing, these areas powered down.

Dr. Newberg also discussed a practice effect. In the beginning of automatic writing, you have to focus, like learning to play the piano, but as the practice becomes more automatic, shall we say, certain parts of the brain begin to power down.

One of the areas that I specialize in with clients is rewiring the subconscious. I call myself an alchemist, meaning I help people transform energy. That's what thought is, energy pinging around inside of us, controlling us without our even knowing it.

Whether our thoughts are coming through meditation, automatic writing, or a trance state, Dr. Newberg said these practices, which take the frontal lobe offline, can potentially provide an opportunity for a person to restructure their mind and how we even think. In essence, the more we're in AWE or a trance-like state, the more we can literally rewire our minds.

The Flow State for Assisting AWE

Ever since Jessica and I developed our program on mindful running (www.MindfulRunning.org), we have been fascinated by the "flow state" also known as "the zone" in sports.

It's a state where time seems to stand still, your mind quiets, and you feel like you can do no wrong, like Michael Jordan or his more recent contemporaries shooting the jumper at the buzzer, just in the nick of time, that wins the game or the championship. In these moments there's no sound, there's no time, just a beingness with the experience.

Now the flow state can come from repetitive motions, from following the breath, from side-to-side movement—there's almost no end to what can put you in this state. For myself, it comes when running, cycling, and especially from skating (you can get in the flow state by following your breath and footfalls when you run, for example).

AWE is another phenomenal tool for getting you in this state. You may find yourself losing track of time, feeling at peace, at one with the world (that's your parietal lobe powering down), and simply in a state of beingness. And while we don't usually associate AWE with movement, there can be an unusual association.

First let me back up, two of my favorite sports are speed skating and skate skiing. You swing from side to side, and that pendulum motion helps put me in the zone, or that flow state. I believe the same motion can take place in AWE. For when I used to use Jessica's old college chair with a huge headrest, my head would sway from side to side. And with all deference to one of the most amazing artists that ever lived, I'd look a bit like Stevie Wonder while I was at the computer keyboard doing AWE (perhaps he was channeling).

Dr. Newberg points out that these movements can put you into that state of flow, or state of AWE. He referred to Sufi dancing when he said, "Whether they are rapid movements, kind of like Sufi dancing, or whether they are slower movements, they can all potentially drive different parts of the brain depending on the circumstances." Oddly enough, it can be small movements as well, so literally picking up a pen can put you in this state too.

It could also be that picking up the pen places the writer on the myelinated superhighway (think of this as the groove in the record of one's mind) toward bliss or a higher state of consciousness.

We've seen people get into a flow state with AWE just by picking up the pen and writing a few prayers. It's as if all of the time spent in AWE had trained the mind to quickly drop the practitioner into this special state.

I asked Dr. Newberg about this, and he said, "When the experienced writers started writing, they would get into this flow state or the parts of the brain powering down much more quickly than others, perhaps even (more than) experienced meditators."

That flow state is what we've been finding in AWE, that when you drop in, you can get into a very deep, plugged-in state, even faster than with meditation. As a near life-long meditator who has spent hour after hour on the cushion, I have never gotten as profound "downloads" or information from the information in my deepest meditations as I have in AWE.

What's really fascinating to me, too, is that meditation is shown to increase frontal lobe activity, while AWE decreases frontal lobe activity. Dr. Newberg's theory is that the difference between the two of these, the "highs and lows" as he calls it, may actually help stimulate profound experiences, awakenings, or even enlightenment experiences.

AWE for Enlightenment?

In a recent interview with Dr. Newberg, we discussed concepts he presents in his book entitled *How Enlightenment Changes Your Brain*. He had this to share:

> When you're flying 500 miles an hour up in the air, when do you feel it? You feel it when you're taking off or when you're landing, because that's where the changes and the shifts are occurring. And so with the brain, it may not necessarily be that the brain is overactive or underactive, but it might be the shift [or the drop] from being overactive to underactive. And in that regard, that may also help us because meditation itself is not enlightenment, but clearly people spend years meditating in order to find enlightenment and that it may be the drop itself and the magnitude of that drop [that could lead to such an experience].
>
> That might make people more likely to have that kind of an experience, much like the airplane analogy. So, I think that there's, some evidence, although it's not 100 percent yet that helps us to start to see how a practice like meditation (or automatic writing) might actually prime the brain for having such an experience.

Since I've known of many people who have mystical experiences in and through AWE, this makes sense. It may be the magnitude of dropping in, particularly coming out of a great meditation, that sends them off on a journey into an "awakening" or "enlightenment" experience.

Now I've never—at least not until now—talked about automatic writing as a path to enlightenment, whatever that may mean, but it does pose an interesting question: can one have a profound, mystical, spiritual experience through AWE, and based on what I've seen, absolutely, yes.

Dr. Newberg and I have discussed the sensory deprivation aspect of AWE—in other words, how shutting down parts of the brain can invoke a spiritual experience. Now in AWE, yes, we have the eyes open a bit to write, and there is theta brain wave entrainment music, but the process is not outwardly focused, or inwardly focused for that matter; it's a complete and total letting go of stimulus—the sensory deprivation.

Have you ever been in a sensory deprivation chamber? Some popular applications are the float pods in which you enter an enclosed shallow salt-water pool or pod that supports you in a buoyant state for thirty minutes or so, in total silence. In these, you are shutting down all sensory input. You may indeed start to experience something otherworldly as your brain perceives something not triggered by sight or sound or feel or hearing.

And that's just what we're looking for in AWE, the perception of the "whatever," beyond the thinking mind. Whether it's from inside or outside, Dr. Newberg doesn't know for certain, but we did discuss the possibility of the brain being a receiver to somewhere else.

When I talk about AWE, I often talk about how it gets easier and easier to hear the voice of AWE, until you don't just hear it when you write, but throughout the day, and I explain this in more detail in chapter 15 about writing without writing. In essence, when you're in AWE you're rewiring the mind.

According to Dr. Newberg, "New neural connections will change over time . . . in [his book] *How Enlightenment Changes Your Brain*, we talk about kind of the more permanent effect of the experience and how people often describe a change in their sense of spirituality, their fear of death, their relationships, their job. So one of the interesting neuroscience questions is that when people have a momentary experience that is profoundly enlightening, is that something that changes the brain in that moment—these experiences often last seconds, maybe minutes, and it seems to radically change a whole person's way of thinking about things."

Speculation is that such experiences may rewire the brain in that moment, in a way, by allowing the brain access to new connections or connections that were always there but were never hooked into the active areas of the brain. So whether these experiences of enlightenment occur over time (such as through meditation practice for hours a day for years or from a momentary experience, even near-death experiences like mine), AWE may predispose the brain to enlightenment.

Dr. Newberg mentioned a study that measured dopamine (a feel-good chemical in the brain). Participants in a spiritual retreat were tested before and after the program. The findings: Their brains handled dopamine differently after the retreat. Some senses were more sensitive to the impact of the dopamine. Did these participants experience some kind of enlightenment as a result of the retreat? Or did these practices prime their brains for having enlightenment?

We can only speculate.

About now, your brain may be hurting as you consider some of the possibilities. So let me throw in a Beatles song for your consideration: "I, Me, Mine." The parietal lobe, the part of the brain that's responsible for self-identification, is what I call the "I, Me, Mine" part. The ego part.

What does this mean other than the song is a classic? That the veteran automatic writing practitioner experiences a greater sense of connectiveness and a decreased sense of self-importance (lower blood flow in imaging in the parietal lobe), or perhaps even in the "ego" or "egoic" part of the brain during automatic writing. And you know I've been explaining the role of ego in AWE.

Perhaps even more fascinating is that, over time, it appears the practitioners (the test subjects in Dr. Newberg's study, as exhibit one) can get into this different brain pattern, or what I'll call a brain wave state, more quickly. We can surmise that ritual and practice help the practitioner get into this state. And it's probably that going into ritual creates new grooves in the record or the mind, making it faster and faster to tap into AWE.

I was hoping that Dr. Newberg would see "spiritual" centers of the brain such as the pineal gland light up—I like to think of the brain as a receiver during automatic writing—but no research specifically into this area has been done yet.

One other key note in general that Dr. Newberg found in his research is that the brains of spiritual practitioners, such as meditators or those who do automatic writing, are 50 percent thicker, than those who do not.

Creativity Comes from Somewhere, but Where?

When we're in a state of AWE, we write differently, perhaps even creating poems, lyrics, or even music, as some of the practitioners have experienced, but I have yet to write a hit song. So from a scientific point of view, the question is where are these thoughts coming from?

Dean Radin, PhD, who is a leading researcher on parapsychology, has some insight for us here. Parapsychology, by the way, is the study of paranormal experiences including near-death experiences, of which I have had two. Despite the common myth that there isn't much evidence to support parapsychology, the reverse is actually true. There's more hard science, data, and statistics to back it up than in almost any other field of science. It's just hard to crack a paradigm steeped in myth that all we are is what we see or that we come from a purely materialistic universe, even though quantum science alone clearly points otherwise. (You can check out several amazing interviews with *Inspire Nation* on this as well with Amit Goswami, PhD, who was featured prominently in the movie *What the Bleep Do We Know!?*) They can be found at www.InspireNationShow.com.

If I were to summarize Dr. Radin's key points, from our interview together, it'd be that any meditative process can help you in all areas of life because the process helps you with focus control. And even more importantly, tapping into an intuitive process like AWE helps cultivate your intuition in all areas of your life and helps that intuition grow beyond merely being accessible in AWE.

Dr. Radin pointed to the work of Daniel Kahneman, PhD, a psychology professor at Princeton, whose landmark book *Thinking, Fast and Slow,* delineates the difference between slow thinking and fast thinking. Fast thinking is this ability to tap into intuition, to get a gut feeling about something or an intuitive hit (which AWE helps cultivate). With slow thinking, you're going to engage all of your analytical skills and get filtered through logic.

Where do those thoughts come from? Dr. Radin speculated that just like with virtually all psychic ability, thoughts bubble up from the unconscious, so when someone is talking about intuition, what they typically mean is they know something without knowing how they know it.

He says there's two types of information percolating up, learned knowledge, even if someone doesn't remember it, like riding a bicycle, and psychic or intuitive hits. And that, "The two are so heavily mixed that it's typically not possible for somebody to know the difference." However, he goes on to say that with practice (such as automatic writing), one can become better at cultivating intuition.

According to Dr. Radin, "If all this stuff is rolling up from the unconscious and you're diving down into that, you're going to get better at it.

Not only better in terms of how it happens spontaneously because you're noticing it, but also better in that you'll be able to consciously access it."

In other words, the more you dive in through a practice like AWE, the better you get at recognizing intuition and the easier to see it popping up. For instance, once you begin recognizing a particular bird call, you start to hear it everywhere.

And the more you tap in and practice seeing it, the easier it is to consciously access it for guidance. It's like getting better communicating with the bird and calling it in yourself.

He also said meditation can improve your ability to tap in. "The deeper you're able to navigate within your own mind, the closer you are to what would normally be considered unconscious."

I asked Dr. Radin if he felt anyone could become a psychic or a channeler. His response? "The question really is could you take a random person who's sort of interested in automatic writing and get them to the point where they become an expert channeler?"

"I would say, yes and no. The yes part is they will get better at it. Certainly, you get better at anything you practice, but it takes talent to get *really* good at anything. And so what's the difference between person A and B? One has talent and the other doesn't [to what extent] we have no idea. Maybe there's a genetic component, or [maybe] there are other components too, we really don't know."

But he says most people (though perhaps not everyone) can improve their psychic abilities and intuitive skills, improving for instance their ability to hear, clairaudience, or see, clairvoyance.

What does all of this mean? That the more you practice and get better at diving down into the unconscious, the more successful and frequently you will be able to consciously access the hidden wisdom within you.

And now you can rest assured that your wisdom and AWE has some basis in science.

8 | Answers to the Big Questions You Have about Automatic Writing

I know you have questions about the automatic writing experience (AWE). I know you may want to change the ritual, the routine, after you've been practicing for some time. I know you wonder if the process is even working.

And that's why this chapter addresses the most-asked questions from practitioners.

I start with the big burning question I am asked in every training session: can I type instead of write? Remember, no rules. Of course you can type. In addition to answers about typing versus writing, I address the use of a special type of journal (or not); but more importantly, we explore the meaning of the words, connecting, and keeping ego at bay.

First, let me share another story, this from Marlene, a practitioner: "My [automatic writing] has taken me soaring to places of happiness and peace," Marlene told me. "I actually sense a oneness with life, nature, the Universe. These are the most fun." She has found in her writing these words: "The stars know me. The mountains know me. The clouds and the wind know me."

She described the process like this: "I drop into a deep self-reflection that challenges me to really know myself and to look deeper into others. I discovered that wisdom when I wrote: 'When your words or beliefs bother me, sometimes I see me hiding in the far recesses of my mirror.'"

My hope is that you can get where Marlene is with her automatic writing. And now answers to your questions.

Can I Use a Keyboard instead of Writing by Hand?

I always recommend starting out writing by hand, although there are a few exceptions. One, if you struggle physically to hold a pen due to arthritis or pain caused by any other disease. Two, if you struggle with hand-eye coordination and struggle to form letters, then go straight to the keyboard.

Note: I'm not talking about penmanship here. Everyone's penmanship suffers with automatic writing, and you will see examples from journals in this book that would make any fourth-grade teacher cringe. How pretty your handwriting is should be the least of your concerns. If your writing is barely legible, then it's a sign you're doing AWE right. A general rule of thumb—the less legible, the better.

And exception three, if you're like me and struggle with dyslexia and flipping words, you may be better off typing.

Truth be told, I do AWE by typing—though I started with writing by hand, which I still recommend as a first step. But here's why I type.

In grade school I had a learning disability. Not only was I diagnosed with hyperactivity, but I physically struggled to handwrite my assignments. I would flip letters around and write them backward. I would jumble my sentences by confusing the order of words and so on. It wasn't until the fourth grade when I was lent an old manual typewriter by Mom did my writing start to take off. And she taped the keys so I couldn't look at the letters and cheat.

In the pre-PC age, I was the first student to master touch typing in my elementary school and the only one who would turn in typewritten assignments at the time. And lo and behold, I started getting straight A's on my writing homework, probably just from the typing alone.

Whether from necessity or preference, you might prefer typing over writing out your AWE. Here are some tips I learned about typing your automatic writing.

Tips for Automatic Writing with a Keyboard

First, I discovered a computer screen on its regular setting is far too stimulating and too bright for us when we are in a half-asleep state in a dark, quiet environment. Aha, a simple solution: dim the blue light.

You can download free software online called f.lux that can help (see Resources). Whether you're a Mac or PC user, the software was designed to dim your screen at night so that you're not overstimulated by blue light, which not only is bad for your eyes, but overactivates your mind while you write.

The software's original design is to filter out the blue light so that you can fall asleep more easily after you've been on your computer and so you have less eyestrain throughout the day. Even if you don't use your computer at night before sleep, look for a built-in feature that dims the blue light to reduce eyestrain. On iPads and iPhones, it's called Night Shift under Settings/Display & Brightness.

I also use a monitor that filters blue light, called a BenQ. This gives me double the blue-light reduction, and my eyes are very happy for this.

As for automatic writing, we want to go beyond blue-light reduction. F.lux has a really cool feature called darkroom mode. Darkroom mode was originally designed for just that, old-school darkrooms so you could be on the computer without exposing the photo film. It allows you to emit almost no visible light by having the screen basically black with red. No white, no blue, no bright colors coming through.

This allows you to type without being overstimulated or jolted by a bright screen. This dimming and color change helps you stay in this half-awake zone while typing with your eyes closed or nearly closed.

Now for myself, I take this to the next level by closing my eyes when I type. I just kick back—fingers typing, eyes closed, head swaying back and forth. I just need to sneak a peek every now and again to make sure my fingers are still on the right keys. Check that there has not been a pop-up window, particularly if you use Google Docs. So you don't discover you've been typing in vain on something like a calendar alert window and there's no record of anything you've written.

And it's just as critical to make sure your fingers are correctly positioned; otherwise, you get vtsxy eritf eotfd nrvusdr youy hinhrtd str noy ppydiyiond yihhy. Kind of like what my kitties would type if they were to walk across my keyboard, as they often do. Technically, there are translators that can sometimes salvage your gibberish, if you've been typing with your finger position off, but it's much better to simply sneak a peek.

Years ago a group coaching client who'd worked for both Google and Apple blew my mind. She suggested typing in Google Docs or, in essence, in the cloud. Getting past the creepiness of having everything online or on Google, I found it magical. Here's why. If you archive your automatic writing, and later you want to see what you said about a particular topic—let's say your business—you can search for keywords and phrases within your documents.

For instance, let's say you remember writing about moving, and you can't recall what you wrote or when. You could do a search on the word "moving" in your Google Docs AWE folder and see what comes up. Or even better, if you had a dream about an eagle, and AWE gave you an amazing interpretation of that dream, and then suddenly you saw an eagle in your waking life, you could go back to your Google Docs and search and find that dream again. So your ability to reference and use what you've written or to look up a dream or idea you had in AWE goes to an entirely new level.

The Downsides to Typing

Here are a few downsides to typing. First, there's an extra step before you can get to your AWE. And sometimes new routines become more difficult to keep up when you start adding extra steps or mental hurdles. Sounds silly, but when you type, you have the added step of turning on your computer or laptop and waiting for it to boot. Then you've got to open your preferred writing application if you didn't leave it open from your last computer session. Whether it's Microsoft Word or Google Docs, you've got to navigate your mouse over to the application, click it, and wait for it to open. Depending on the speed of your computer and your tech savviness, this can add a few minutes to your process.

But if you're handwriting in your journal, like Jessica does, all you have to do is flip open your journal and click your pen. She gets going nearly instantaneously. In fact, she doesn't even move from our bed. She wakes up, maybe makes a quick trip to the bathroom, returns, meditates, and starts writing all in the same cocoon where she slept. It doesn't get much easier than that.

With any device that has internet connectivity, there is the allure of checking your email, social media, the news or whatever dings, rings, or pops up a notification to pull your attention away. If this happens, not only are you waking yourself up, but depending on what you've read, you're potentially completely derailing your mind in the process. Make sure your notifications are turned off the evening before.

Jessica is a fast typist, but she gets the deepest, most profound words of wisdom when she writes rather than types. So I recommend you try the writing first. See how that goes. Give it a good thirty-day test—and make a commitment to yourself. That's a key to success if you're making that handshake on a daily basis.

Frankly, there's something magical about the touchy-feely kinesthetic process of having your pen in hand and scrawling your hand across the paper. I find it much easier initially to get into AWE this way, and there's something more creative to me about having that tactile sensation of pen to paper and seeing the words literally flow onto the page. When I do, boy, does it look like a mess—but still, it feels so good.

There is also something cool about creating physical matter out of thin air. And by this I mean filling pages and journals through the process of AWE. It feels so tangible and real that looking back at them, thumbing through the pages, can be a mystical experience unto itself.

A final downside to typing is this: one of the magical occurrences with writing with pen and paper takes place when your writing hand crosses over your body's centerline over and over again. This movement is said to help you bridge the hemispheres of your brain and get you further in the flow or the zone. Obviously, this crossing-the-midline magic doesn't exactly occur when you are typing on a keyboard.

Try out typing and see if it works for you. Some people do much better on the keyboard. On the other hand, you might find after a week or two it's not for you and you want to go back to the touchy-feely, more kinesthetic experience of a pen and a journal.

Both methods of writing—handwriting or typing—can have the same outcome, and we can look at both sides of the coin and see possibilities. However, I do feel that there is a richness to the handwritten word, that there is an energy, an energetic imprint with putting words on paper that we don't get or can lose in the digital experience, which is why I'm always going to default and say write by hand if at all possible—at least give it a few weeks before you head to the keyboard.

Do I Need a Special Journal?

I highly recommend a really fun journal. Jessica has a heavy, leather-bound journal with carved dragons on the cover. Dragons! How does it get any better than this? And when you're writing with dragons, or whatever feels good to you, it's as if you are writing spells into a book of magic—like a book plucked from a *Lord of the Rings* or *Harry Potter* library.

Of course, you don't have to use something fancy. And I'm not a consumerist by nature. I'd rather be more eco, so something with many pages, vegan, and even better with recycled paper suits me best. I've even been known to use those familiar black-and-white composition notebooks. Of course mine would feature puppies on the cover and be eco-friendly. Economical or extravagant. Space age or vintage. A legal pad. Lined or unlined. It's all up to you.

Ritual is important to the subconscious. So I recommend choosing a writing material that speaks to you. Grab your favorite pen too. The beauty of having a journal is that you can do AWE just about anywhere, while traveling, while away, in the woods, near a lake, on a mountain top. No boot-up time.

Think of your journal as something sacred, precious, special. Jessica's leather-bound dragon journal has a hefty, thick hard cover. Since she does the majority of her AWE in bed or at home, in general, its weight and size isn't an inconvenience. To Jessica, having a journal that takes up substantial space is symbolic of how much she values her AWE practice. You too may feel compelled to pick up a special journal, or you might be just as satisfied with a 99-cent purse- or pocket- or backpack-sized notebook. AWE works just as well either way.

However, the more you invest in AWE, either financially or emotionally, the more likely you are to keep up the practice.

AWE practitioner Dr. Kapil Shripad Apshankar said, "I am very, very picky about the writing supplies I use. I mostly use a fountain pen. I have about four inked up at any given time. Alternatively, I will use a glitter gel pen with a broad line. Another important must-have for me is blank, unruled paper in landscape mode. That's the only way I will write. The blank, unruled paper in landscape mode is like my canvas. A canvas for creating my dream life, and also a canvas for me to communicate with the Divine. It is in this space that inspiration flows, easily and effortlessly."

How Do I Know If AWE Is Working?

Other than the mechanics of writing or typing and the journal itself, this is the question most practitioners ask, and I am happy to answer.

In the beginning, you may only get small sentence fragments or snippets, or you might not get anything at all. That's all right, both because it's a process or you could say a practice, and it will come with time. And because you'll likely find yourself feeling better even before the words start flowing.

Almost everyone gets AWE within a month, and many from day one. Here's approximately how it breaks down. Typically, about 10 percent of people start getting the most incredible poetry, prose, or lyrics, almost on day one. I still don't get deep poetry or music, I have no idea how they do it. The next 10 percent get profound, deep words of wisdom in the beginning, just not Shakespearean prose. Then the majority of people, about 60 percent, get almost nothing to begin with, just tiny little snippets or sentence fragments. That's fine too.

Finally, the remaining 10 to 20 percent of people don't get anything for the first few weeks, but they start to feel better anyway. That's because AWE goes beyond the words, it's a frequency and a connection you're building with your inner wisdom or guides, and that connection often grows much stronger, even before there are words.

The entire next chapter is devoted to addressing this question of whether AWE is working in much more depth.

When I put out the word to practitioners that I was looking for examples of their AWE writing for this book, I received the pages you see reprinted in this book. I also received some poetry. The authors of the following poems graciously agreed to let me share them.

For goodness sake
For goodness sake
Why can't we see
That kindness is
The way to be
When we're upset
We all should try
To let our anger
Monster die
To show the ones
We love the best
We care enough

To let it rest
So practice kindness
Each new day
In all we think
And do and say
  —Jeff Harmening

Fire of child, child of fire
raising the energy from dead wood
raising the heat in the making
raising gods as the trail begins
walking in pace with all things
surrendering to love and light
bring forth our missions to the eternal
this valley is in our souls
our souls are in this valley
we will never own you
please free us as we go
  —Emilien Reynal

How Do I Know What to Write?

For years when I did automatic writing, I would just keep repeating my invocation prayer until words started popping in or saying, *I don't know what to write, I don't know what to write, I don't know what to write.* Basically writing gibberish and that too is part of the process.

Once you finish your prayer and ask for your highest good, start in. The writing may flow like this: *I don't know what to write. I don't know what to write. Write is my white and write and bright light*—and just keep the pen going. Let it be nonsensical. Let it be gibberish. Don't think about what you should write. Just keep the pen going.

These days I quite frequently tell people to literally write junk—meaning nonsensical words, phrases, sentences, anything to get you writing without the involvement of the thinking mind.

Some clients start writing prayer. Then the words would pop in. What we don't want to do is think about what's coming next or accidentally ask ourselves for the answers. Even if you do five to ten minutes and you get complete nonsense—and that's rare with the exception of maybe a little bit in the first few weeks—you will feel different because you've now created that cosmic handshake with something up above, so to speak, or with your deepest inner wisdom.

Just keep writing.

One of my students, Ryan, said, "I sometimes find if I am stuck, if I just repeat a sentence over and over it frees up the subconscious. For example, this morning I repeated *I am able to accomplish anything I choose. I joyfully release the past and expect the best now and in the future.*"

For me, when I was stressed about my program, scheduling guests, writing this book, and I turned to AWE, and asked what I needed to know, I got this: *Relax, Michael. We've got your back. It's all going to be taken care of.*

For the newbie to AWE, I recognize your feelings. You feel uncomfortable. Awkward even. It should feel uncomfortable, it should feel awkward, it should feel weird, it should feel contrived, it should feel false, it may even feel fake.

You'll want to stop. You'll say to yourself, "This isn't working." Just like I did in my early AWE attempts when I disregarded the message about speaking to millions from a mountain top. I felt the messages were a fraud. As it turned out, they were not.

In other words, it is not natural at the beginning and so you're not going to feel like, I'm surrounded by angels and there's love everywhere and there's rose petals floating in air. Well, it's possible, but for most people it's a bit more subtle. Like you, they are thinking, Am I doing this right? This is really weird. I'm uncomfortable. How in the world will I know if it's coming from me. This is silly. I'm almost embarrassed that I'm actually doing this.

Perfect. That means your mind is wondering or worrying about whether you're doing a good job rather than your mind actually creating the words on the page. Absolutely perfect.

Now when you reread your work, amid the gibberish, you might find some gems: *You are loved, you're loved. It's all good. It's all okay.* Then, you went back to, *I don't know what to write, I don't know what to write. This feels weird, this feels silly, this feels foolish. Why am I doing this? You are loved. This feels foolish, this feels silly.* You go back and you reread it and you see the tiny little snippets that may come off the page.

Later on, after the words begin to flow—sometimes a few days to a few weeks, you may feel, Oh, my God. This feels so amazing. I don't want to stop. That is why it is a state of awe, why it is awesome, why it is the AWE experience because it's so incredible. Just like with meditation, don't get attached to any particular outcome. It's not a bad day of AWE if you sat down, didn't get anything, and then got a to-do list. Okay, it's not quite an AWE experience. But that time sitting with AWE whether or not profound wisdom comes to you is still as good as gold.

The more writing you do, however, the more the words will flow and the profound wisdom will chase you down. For myself, the words come before I even have a chance to get my prayers down. I still get them down to be safe, but the more you practice, the faster you'll get into AWE and the deeper you'll go down the rabbit hole.

My student Sodani shared this story:

> I went into this program with no expectations, but simply
> with an open heart and an eagerness to offer that heart back
> to the one who created it. The ever-devoted student, I followed
> Michael's directions to a T, even writing out the protection
> and invocation prayers when I wasn't even sure I completely
> believed them. For weeks and weeks, I wrote. When I would
> read back the words, all I heard was my own voice speaking
> back to me (albeit a kind, encouraging voice). I felt a little dis-
> couraged because I was hoping for some profound wisdom to
> be bestowed upon me for my faithful dedication. Even so, I
> kept writing. This practice even inspired me to start convers-
> ing with Source throughout the day.
>
> And then seemingly out of the blue, as Michael promised,
> something miraculous happened. Source responded back. Not
> directly in my writing per se, but as little sparks of inner know-
> ings. As I would think a question during the day, not directly
> aiming it at anyone in particular, the answer would instanta-
> neously arrive at my heart's doorstep, wrapped up neatly with
> a shiny bow. I wasn't sure AWE would work for me, but I was
> graciously proven wrong. AWE is pure magic.

There are exceptions to every rule. Some people have put pen to
paper and almost from word one they get, *We've been waiting for you,
Michael.* And you're thinking, Oh, my God, and then boy do they have
words to share.

Don't take just my word for it. Here is what another practitioner
told me about her automatic writing experience: It was January 2018.
Helen said she was feeling spiritually depleted and very disconnected.

In her words, "I was so busy with the routine of work and maybe the dark days of deep winter contributed to my overall malaise (I live in Buffalo, New York), I don't know, but I did know that I needed something. I had been listening to *Inspire Nation* frequently and always found it uplifting (WOO HOO!) and when Michael mentioned AWE and how it had been a tremendous influence in his life, I thought, Well, why not? So I got the (AWE online) course and began writing."

She said, "I pretty much devoured it! The very first writing session was amazing, and I felt like I had reconnected with a spiritual part of me that had lain dormant for years. I wrote every day, sometimes twice a day, and filled a huge notebook, front to back, with what I call messages from my Angels. Now its 2020 and I haven't written as much as in those first few months, but I absolutely know that my Spirit helpers are with me all the time, and I do not ever feel disconnected. AWE helped open up a path for me that included extensive meditation and breathwork, hot yoga and mindfulness. I feel like I was guided to AWE and that it was a new beginning in my spiritual evolution."

How Do I Know if It's My Ego Writing?

Automatic writing always comes from a loving, kind, supportive place. Your inner wisdom or guides have no judgment nor ill will, only love. Despite everything that your ego has shouted at you all these years, your inner wisdom still loves you—Universe, angels, God, guides, Buddha, Allah, everybody still loves you too.

When you're writing from your higher self, your writing will reflect that, it's a kind, gentle, loving voice. Like a loving parent who'll do anything for their child.

At times, your writing can be a stern voice, particularly if it's coming from a mentor, like my mentor Jack, who's on the other side. I can still hear him saying, in person, and in automatic writing, *Dammit Michael, take better care of that baby doll* (Jessica). It's from a place of love, but he's serious. And I'm on it!

However, even when that voice is stern, it's like a parent holding a newborn child. It's coming 100 percent out of love, with absolutely no judgment at all. It simply wants what's best for you and for the highest good of all.

If, instead of a loving voice, you're getting woulda, coulda, shoulda or as I like to joke, getting "shoulded" all over such as, *Michael, why didn't you do this? Michael, why didn't you do that?* or more to the point of, *Oh, I shoulda done this or that. If only I'd done that. When is this going to happen?* then that is worry, fear and concern, or judgment. It's not AWE. That's your ego.

Here's the crazy thing. That's okay too. That's actually really cool. Because your ego is here to serve you. I don't believe in eliminating ego, destroying ego, or even rising above ego. Because your ego is a part of you. It's here to serve you, to guide you, and once you make peace and integrate your ego, ego can be your new best friend. I think of ego as your wounded inner child. When you listen to ego and help her or him to heal, you'll feel much better.

Of course, you'll never want to give ego the keys to your RV, but you'll be happier with ego riding shotgun. So how do you turn the voice of ego into a positive? Quite simply, when ego comes up, we're going to let ego know we'll be with him or her in just a short minute, and I explained how you park ego in the backseat of the car. And let ego hang out there, because if ego knows that they are going to be heard, they'll camp out and wait. Maybe they'll pop up briefly once or twice more, but just lovingly ask ego to wait.

I explained the process of the Ego Dump in chapter 3, and I refer you there if you need to revisit the technique on how to park ego in the backseat.

Who Can I Connect with in AWE?

I must admit, before I began automatic writing, I wasn't much of an angels or archangels guy. I knew something saved my life, and not just twice, but from the many, many accidents I'd been in, and many more I'd just avoided. I assumed it was angels or guardian angels, but it wasn't until I looked into it all that I understood the full extent of who or what was by my side.

In the beginning I really had no intention of connecting with any particular beings other than my source of inner wisdom. Now I've discovered an entire entourage of guides I can count on to support me. They run the gamut from angels to spirit animals and even to deceased loved ones.

When I started automatic writing, I had this special urge to write to the archangels and to three in particular. I didn't know what they stood for, or why to write to them, but I felt a calling, and I heeded it.

Let me introduce you to my fab three:

Archangel Michael. He's my favorite angel to call in, and not just because of his name. But because I picture him with a giant sword of quartz and light. He cuts through the darkness, keeps me safe, and helps clear the path for my safety, guidance, and greatest future. According to angel expert Kyle Gray, Michael is "the king of angels, and the patron saint of protection." He is the go-to angel to call on in times of need for strength, guidance, and protection.

Archangel Raphael. He's my second go-to angel, and his main power is healing. He helps me heal clients of both physical and emotional trauma, along with any energetic patterns or wounds that are keeping them stuck. He's also the angel to go to in times of turmoil and travel and when I'm feeling ungrounded.

Archangel Gabriel. She is the angel of nurturing and guidance, the one who helps me heal my inner wounds, connect with my inner child, and has a soft yet powerful, loving presence. When I'm suffering, struggling, or needing self-forgiveness, I call on Archangel Gabriel, and she'll be by my side. She's also the angel to call on when I'm struggling with communication, hearing my truth, or getting my voice out there.

I feel something profound when I write to these archangels. And if I take the time in AWE—or even when I call them in before an interview—I feel them and know they're there, ready and waiting to support me.

They've been my protectors, my guides, my healing light, and just about everything else you can think of. They've been my muses, my north star, certainly my teachers, and when I've gotten out of line, they've been there to reel me in as well and set me straight.

So I cannot recommend going to the angels or archangels enough. You don't have to call in "mine" (of course they're all of ours), but choose whomever or whichever you resonate with.

You may be wondering about the difference between angels and archangels. In simple terms the archangels are the top of the food chain, and then regular angels are beneath them. There are many other categories such as guardian angels, whom we're not only born with, but are here with us for each and every incarnation. For myself, Maximilian, who takes the form of a mountain lion is one of my guardian angels. I write to him daily for protection and guidance, and he's always by my side.

For myself, if I take the time and go slowly with each angel I call in, I feel a shiver going from my arms and down my spine, a brush of what feels like feathers against my skin, I suppose what could be thought of as angel wings. Angel expert Kyle Gray calls these "angel bumps."

So if I call in Archangel Michael and pause, I feel this brush or tingly sensation, then I'll call in the next archangel and pause and wait to feel something, and so on. I can even feel a brush or tingling sensation when I call in my deceased pet Molé as well. (I dive into connecting with loved ones on the other side in a later chapter.)

How Do I Know Who's Writing to Me?

In simplest terms, I'd ask during AWE, "Which guide or angel am I speaking with?" or "Who are my guides?"

For myself, if I write specifically to one angel, or guide, such as my power animal and protector, the lion Maximilian, he'll personally write back. However, if I ask generically, I rarely get the answer I am looking for. Sometimes I get an angel, or Mother Earth, but often it's very generic. But I don't worry about it, because I've prayed to the highest level, surrounded myself in love and light, and the most glorious, loving, kind, and guiding words are there for me to read.

9 | Help! AWE Is Not Working— What Am I Doing Wrong?

As promised, I address in greater detail the concern that some practitioners feel and that's whether their automatic writing experience (AWE) is working. But first I ask, are you sure, absolutely sure, your automatic writing is not working?

Interestingly enough, many people get profound words of wisdom in the beginning, even without realizing it. This is for two reasons. First, we want to be half awake, and so you may not even recall what you've written after you're done. That's why it's so important to go back and reread what you've written.

Second, we often get snippets in the beginning, and each snippet on its own doesn't mean much. But when you read them back all together, you may get a general idea of what's being said, and you just might find some profound words of wisdom. This is quite common. Or at least a feeling that your inner wisdom is there, working on speaking with you.

Reread Your Writing

What do I write, what do I write, I don't know what to write, loved, love, dear one love, I don't know what to write, I don't know what to write, all is good, I don't know what to write, I don't know what to write, relax, I don't know what to write, supported, I don't know what to write, good.

On their own, these words from AWE might not mean much, although it might be clear that you are loved from someone or something, but if you put them all together, loved, love, dear one love, all is good, relax, supported, good, you get the general idea that you, dear one, are loved, that all is good, that you can relax, you're supported, and all is well.

Even in the beginning, AWE is a healing process. Whether it comes from words, phrases, snippets, or just the energy of being in AWE, your stress levels go down, your joy for life starts to go up, or your depression starts to lift, and you begin to feel much better.

When you're writing in AWE, you are experiencing a healing process. You feel lighter, you feel better about yourself. Like me, you may feel darkness being taken away just from getting into this process.

Some of my coaching clients have had profound experiences almost from day one. Poems come through, as I shared in the last chapter, and others get words of wisdom from people who have passed on, guidance that they never would have expected. Sometimes a switch flips on and the floodgates open. Followed by nothing. That's perfectly all right as well.

Trina, for example, was delighted to receive a birthday message from her inner voice. As she tells it, "It's my birthday today, and as I have been doing for the past couple of weeks, I got up and did my automatic writing, and this was the last thing my guides gave me, which just tickled me, and I wanted to share."

> We'd recommend that you up your tolerance for Bliss because there's a blissload of it coming your way and you don't want it to run over and squash you but make the trip to Bliss land more speedily and the ability to make the whole world the way you want simply by wanting the world the way that it is.

"I am grateful grateful grateful," she told me.

Trina shared a birthday message she received in AWE.

So read back the words that you're given—the words that came out on paper and see what you've got.

Whenever I teach automatic writing, I always have my clients review AWE later in the day. Why? Because when we're in a state of AWE, we're half awake, and half here and half not. So we rarely remember what we wrote.

That's good. It means your thinking mind was disengaged or taken out of the puzzle or basically had a pillow over it, so rereading those words later on can be eye-opening. When we assume nothing useful, let alone profound, has come through AWE, we're quite surprised by what we read later on. You'd be surprised how many times you'll react with, "Wow, I had absolutely no idea" or "I didn't know I could be so deep or so wise."

Many a client has told me, "Michael, I'm not getting anything out of it. It's just gibberish. Nothing's making sense."

And I ask, "Would you mind sharing a bit of your writing with me?"

They start reading and their jaw hits the floor. Because they can see how profound a few of the words were that came out. They read it and marvel. They might say, "Is that what I think I just said?"

"Yes, exactly," I tell them.

We find they were given guidance for the day, or their lives, or even words of love and encouragement from a deceased loved one. Profound words come up, sneaking in between all of the scribbling of *I have no idea what to write. Why am I even doing this kind of thing?*

On the subject of guidance, Lynda shared this story:

> When I started AWE, I had just rescued an older dog from a harsh situation with an unethical breeder. She was in pretty rough shape. I was seriously concerned that she had major medical issues that would not be curable, and that I would not be able to bond with her and bring her out of her shell. As I started writing each morning, I received messages of encouragement, and I was told in no uncertain terms that she would be fine, and that I would be able to solve her health issues (specifically digestive) with a little guidance. I took her to the vet, had all of her tests done and her medical needs attended to, but her digestive issues persisted.
>
> During a subsequent AWE session, I was given instructions to give her raw food with some pro- and prebiotics. Within days, she was eating and gaining weight! I was flabber-

gasted to say the least. She has fully regained her health and has become a wonderful, affectionate canine companion.

In retrospect, every piece of guidance I've received during AWE has been spot on, and I've come to fully trust the process and I now feel divinely guided and fully supported in my life.

So after you do your AWE, make sure you reread it at least once during the day. While I used to recommend midday, I now also recommend right before going to sleep. For there's a special energy, or resonance to your writing, and when you reread it before bedtime, it helps put you in a special, sacred place. To me, bedtime is ceremony, for you're about to walk through a doorway to another world for six to eight hours or more. What could be more sacred, or set you up for a better journey, than rereading your AWE?

You feel better and at greater peace, and AWE helps you have a better night's sleep, or even better dreams while you sleep, almost as if you're back in that state of AWE or connection with the Universe while you sleep.

What If Automatic Writing's Still Not Working?

If you're struggling to get into AWE, or the words just aren't flowing, do not despair. There are many things you can do to switch things up and find what works. So let me address some ways to experiment and try a different technique.

After all, if the process is not yet working for you (or you think it's not working), think of this chapter as a troubleshooting manual like the one that came with your new lawn mower. We'll check the gas, the oil, set the height adjustment, and hope we can pull the starter and hear the motor roar.

First, I'd look at when you're writing. Often any challenge at all with AWE is cleared up once you start writing a little bit earlier. Often we're just too influenced by the sound and energy of those around us. Try getting up earlier.

Get in the AWE Zone

Earlier I talked about there being a field of energy that surrounds us, that perfuses us, and that we're in essence swimming in. It's an energetic field of everyone else's thoughts and nervous energy, or it could be their positive energy too.

The challenge occurs when that energy's overwhelming, or too close to us, and then can shut AWE down. So we need an AWE zone or safety zone where others aren't affecting our field. This means looking for a quiet place in the house, away from the kids, away from your spouse, and away from anyone else's energy. If need be, it could be the bathroom, the basement, the closet, and I've even seen people go out to their car—even if it's in the garage in order to write. Find or create this sacred space, and you'll find it much easier to write.

If the time isn't the issue, often the location is, if we're too close to others, not comfortable, or in a stimulating environment, this can shut down the flow.

You Are Where You Vibrate

Simply put, you aren't just your energy, nor the energy of your friends and their friends, but you are the energy of everyone around you, or everyone in your energetic field. And this field can extend out, way out. According to researchers like Howard Martin, the coauthor of *The HeartMath Solution*, and Dean Radin, PhD, chief scientist at the Institute of Noetic Sciences, and those working on the Global Coherence Initiative, we're each tuning forks, and together we create a field around our home, our cities, our countries, and even the entire planet.

Therefore, when you are in an environment where everybody is stressed out, you are stressed out. That's why so many of my clients have been hard pressed to get a great night's sleep during these challenging pandemic times—and why we made a program just for that, called the Magical Evening Routine (www.MagicalEveningRoutine.com).

With that said, for whatever reason, and there are often plenty of reasons, people are waking up in the middle of the night because the field is freaked out, which becomes a feedback loop—the more freaked out you are, the more people feel your vibration, and the more their nervous system goes into fight or flight, and now they're freaked out too. Then your nervous system notices they're freaking out, and you take your freak out to an entirely new level.

Welcome to the age of COVID and beyond, whatever lies out there for us. The AWE training in this book will help you move past the freak-out and help you to be the calmest, coolest tuning fork in your town, helping literally to transform the lives of those around you.

If you are doing your automatic writing when everybody is running down the road to get to work instead of tapping into your inner wisdom, you're tapping into the "I've got to get to work" energy in your external environment. And if they're freaked out about their boss, or day ahead, then you are too. This is why we don't feel entirely safe, even when we're working from home, because we can feel that freaked-out field of energy all around us.

If you feel your home or the surrounding area is sabotaging your automatic writing, try to find another location that's safe and quiet, such as a library, a meditation center, a yoga studio, a quiet room in your workplace, a garden setting, a study carrel, a park, a trail, in a kayak in the middle of a serene lake, a classroom when all the students have left.

Declutter Your Environment

We're not just energetically sensitive to the people around us but to all of the stuff that surrounds us as well. Look at the clutter around you, in your environment, in your home. If you're trying to automatic write in a soup of clutter, you may not have the success you seek.

Just as it's important to write before people wake up, particularly near the city, it's important to have a clutter-free environment, no matter how small it is, to write from as well. Because everything has an energy. A rock has an energy, a dirty dish has an energy, and that laundry that's been on the floor for days has an energy. So ask yourself how chaotic is your environment? Can you clear it, put things away? Or can you get away from it? Either inside your home or elsewhere?

Do what you can to find a space that's not just quiet from a noise perspective, but from a clutter perspective as well. This is also why you don't want to dwell on the N.E.W.S.—what I call "negative worthless stimulation" or bring too much of it into your environment, because you'll begin vibrating with it as well.

Therefore, we need to find an energetically quiet place, devoid of clutter, of zany people, and of anything else that may be stimulating or overstimulating you and making it hard to get into AWE.

It's why we're very lucky and always try to find places to live where we can stare out at the countryside and melt into the scenery. You might not be able to do that quite literally, but perhaps you can set up a room, or a part of a room, or even part of a closet as a small "shrine" from which to do your AWE.

Look critically at your internal environment in your home and surrounding area and ask what you can do to improve it, upgrade it, or declutter it, to improve your time in AWE.

And if you're fortunate enough like myself, challenge yourself over time to look for a place in the world for you and your family that vibrates more in alignment with how you'd like to feel. Particularly through AWE (and we'll cover manifestation in a later chapter), you can help draw yourself to almost anything, or any place you desire in life. As an energetic being, if you can feel it, then you can achieve it.

Fine-Tune Your AWE Ritual

- **Avoid email, the news, social media, even online shopping, or any other mental stimulants before writing.** Constant scrolling and watching can short-circuit the mind, trigger a fight-or-flight response, and definitely keep you out of AWE.
- **Make sure you've done your morning meditation before AWE.** Often people say that they wanted to get into the writing first, and then do the meditation. My recommendation is to follow everything in order, exactly as described, before veering off. Is it possible to write in AWE without meditation? Yes, after significant practice where you can tune in at the drop of a hat. But even for myself, AWE goes much deeper if I've taken the time to step away from my mind.
- **Continue the prayers.** Actually, this is often the number-one reason people struggle. They start with the prayers for the first few days and then stop writing them, or just read them out loud. But the prayers serve as more than a way to call in assistance,

they're also to help step you down into the rabbit hole, like Alice in Wonderland, or like going into self-hypnosis. So do not skip the prayers. Once you start writing the prayers, keep writing them. Always.

Tinker and Experiment

In essence, when it comes to problem-solving, we want to go back to the basics first, and then explore and expand from there. As Occam's razor states, the simplest solution is probably the answer. So go back to basics first and foremost.

Here are some other techniques for you to try:

- **Turn up the music.** Often simply dialing up the volume knocks your brain offline and helps you get into that state of AWE. You can also listen to different binaural theta brain-entrainment music selections. Just make sure they are labeled as theta.
- **Try a different pen or a different journal.** Again, I like going as tactile as you can. You could even try an old-school fountain pen, it certainly sets the ambiance.
- **Try typing.** I always prefer it when people save this strategy for later, but if you're tripping over your words, reversing letters, or generally just downright frustrated with your writing, then it's time to clack the keys. I know that's what I had to do, though I was first able to connect with AWE in my handwriting—I just couldn't keep up.
- **Try different positions.** Sit in a different chair. Or on the floor. Or near a different window. For myself, chairs matter. I am most comfortable, as I said, in Jessica's old, beat-up college chair.
- **Move to a different space.** Go to another room, a closet, the garage, a car, or even a sacred space outside—one where you

won't be people watching or disturbed or stimulated in any way. Each room and place has a different energy.

- **Consider a different type of meditation.** And do your best to let go, rather than work hard during the meditation.
- **Experiment with different prayers.** One client of mine just kept writing and rewriting St. Francis of Assisi's prayer until other words came through. It was a brilliantly creative strategy that rewarded him with AWE.

Let Go

Don't try to force the practice of automatic writing. In many ways AWE is uncannily similar to dating, in that we never find the one we're looking for when we're trying too hard. It's when we relax and let go that "the one" often magically appears. I know Jessica did in this way.

You can also think of AWE like *trying* to fall asleep, which never works. When we try to fall asleep, we stimulate the mind and the fight-or-flight response, and we can do anything BUT fall asleep. It's only when we let go, give up, and just relax into the moment, or into the mattress, that suddenly we open our eyes, and it's morning. The same can be said for AWE.

Step back, relax in, but do not try to force it. Over time, for everyone, AWE does come, it may just take time. So breathe deeply and, in all seriousness, play with AWE. The more you take it as a fun task, a cool experiment, or even a game, the sooner AWE will come through. Don't make it work, and don't take it seriously, we've got enough seriousness in life to worry about as is.

It goes without saying—but I'll say it anyway—change only one part of the ritual at a time. Otherwise, if you change many parts, you won't know which one made a difference.

* * *

As you experiment with various places, techniques, and methods to surrender into AWE, let me again emphasize that I recommend a thirty-day practice, which I explain in more detail in chapter 14 and the 30-Day Challenge, because everybody over time who's kept with it has gotten words of wisdom. They are there inside you. It's not magic. It's your inner wisdom.

When we keep doing the automatic writing experience, wisdom comes for all of us. So don't worry and think, "Oh, I'm not an enlightened master." Neither am I, nor do you have to be. And you certainly don't have to be the Michael Jordan of channeling in order to be able to get this. There's no ranking. There's no judgment. Just keep practicing and it will come. I promise.

Your hurdles are not really hurdles at all but normal and natural feelings and thoughts as you refine your practice. The next chapters help you go higher (or deeper) and refine your practice, just as you can lean into a stretch in yoga, you can lean into automatic writing to mine different answers and experiment with other techniques. I'll show you how.

10 | How to Get Unstuck and Get Your Life Back on Track with Automatic Writing

Looking at the world around me—and the lives of my clients and class participants, particularly during this time—it appears people are more stuck than ever. We feel in a rut, helpless, hopeless, don't know where to turn or how to kick-start our lives again.

This is one area where AWE (the automatic writing experience) can help tremendously, for it can help us step back, look big picture at our lives, find the golden thread, and see the direction forward. Heck, like a car being stuck in the mud, it'll even give you a good healthy push or boost to help move you forward.

I know when Jessica and I left Maui after getting our butts kicked, I felt stuck and at the same time knew it was short term. Why? Because I had just started the practice of automatic writing and knew the answers would come. And boy did they! AWE told us to start the *Inspire Nation* show, how to get the coaching business going again, and how to navigate each and every step that led us to our dream home in Colorado.

Whenever I feel stuck and I go into AWE, I'm transported into a world of limitless possibilities and am shown some powerful steps to take from right where I am. In essence, my inner wisdom, angels, and guides show me exactly where I am, why I'm here, and where to go from here.

Find Your Purpose, Path, and Direction with AWE

One of the absolute, most important and powerful ways to use automatic writing is for discovering what I call your PPD—or your purpose, path, and direction.

Not only can you ask, "What do I need to know today?" and "Who am I?" but you can ask questions like the following:

- "Where do I want to go in life?"
- "What's a great path for me?"
- "What are my passions?"
- "What are my hopes and dreams on a soul level?"
- "What is the mission I came here with?"

Or something that I talk about on the show often and in coaching is this question:

"Can you help me develop my mission statement and discover my true purpose in life?"

The automatic writing experience will help you get this big-picture perspective of your entire life and what you're here to do on a spiritual, soul level.

I encourage you to ask often: "What's my purpose, path, and direction?" "Where am I going in life?" "What was I brought here for?" "What is my mission?" "Why did I choose this incarnation?"

You get more clarity, and with more clarity comes direction to help guide you through your life. You could also ask about patterns, about pitfalls: "Why do I keep repeating this pattern?" "Why do I keep shooting myself in the foot?"

If you are concerned with the answer to this question, "Why do these emotions keep coming up in me?" then ask about them and you'll get guidance. You'll also get learnings from AWE that will help you be able to clear blockages, to let them go and take different actions.

In any area where there are emotions involved, where there are repeating patterns, if you feel emotionally stuck, withdrawn, depressed, sad, anxious, or scared—and the list goes on and on and on—bring it to automatic writing and ask for guidance. You will be amazed at the response. Some of my client stories can help explain.

I once worked with John, a famous painter. His artistic work went for tens of thousands of dollars, but at the time I met him, he felt lost and stuck. He had a habit of building up a business and then tanking it. We had to learn why. Fortunately, he took up automatic writing and began to get answers.

He discovered a fear of inadequacy, of not being enough, and even confusion of where he wanted to go in life. However in AWE it all became clear. He was able to stop the self-sabotage, get a rhythm to his day, and fully embody his work.

To do this, AWE and I (we tag-team in coaching) encouraged him to take pauses and bring the joy back into his life. And when he did, his business took off. We also encouraged him to front-load doing the things first that he feared or regretted most—this was a challenge for him, as he'd often start projects and have a hard time finishing them. Once he started following through on projects, his business took off to an entirely new level.

Mary Bell was an executive. She was struggling to figure out where she wanted to go in life. She was an immigrant, and quite successful at what she did, but she always felt a bit like a fish out of water. Then she began working with AWE. And while the answers didn't come to her all at once, she started getting more and more clarity.

She thought she wanted to leave her job and become a counselor. However, the more she asked AWE, the more things in her life began to switch. Not only did she realize she already was a counselor at work—just not an official one—but she began to make peace with her work. And as she did so, her life began to radically change. She received one promotion after another.

Now she's at least three if not four major rungs up the corporate ladder, overseeing massive teams above the level she was working at when she started into AWE. And even her boss's boss now works for her. And while she, too, doesn't know exactly what's coming next in the world, through AWE she knows she's exactly where she's supposed to be.

Mired in Energy Soup

Everything is about energy. In my regular coaching work, I consider myself an alchemist, not meaning I can literally transform lead into gold—wouldn't that be nice. But meaning that I help people transform negative energy into positive energy, and hopes and dreams into reality. We are all swimming in a sea or soup of energy, as I have indicated earlier, and when we learn how to work with it, we can "tai chi" the energy as I like to call it, or take it in, swirl it around, and turn it into something incredibly positive in our lives.

We are all energetic beings (according to quantum science, we are all energy, and there's no separation between anything and anyone).

In essence, we're all made of molecules and the molecules are made of atoms, and it turns out that the atoms are simply frequency vibrating in a field. Everything is frequency vibrating in a field, and there is no separation between these frequencies, anywhere. And since we're made of energy, and vibrate as energy, it makes sense that we're all energetically sensitive, even if we don't realize it.

It's fascinating, when the inhabitants of the International Space Station look down on the United States, they see glowing lights along the East Coast. The highways and cities, the pockets of people, a soup of light. And we exist in that soup. And it's not just light, it's energy. The energy of love, such as on Christmas, the energy of fear, such as before a massive election, or almost any Monday morning for that matter.

We all are human tuning forks. We vibrate with whatever is around us. Go to a rock concert and you'll literally feel yourself vibrate. Stand outside a church bell tower, and once an hour (or more) you'll feel the vibrational energy as well. We've all felt it whether listening to good music, or bad music, a good speaker, or a terrible one. And we've all felt a vibration when someone special comes into the room. I haven't met the Dalai Lama yet, but I have to imagine, when he comes into the room, there's a palpable vibration.

I used to have a special meditation teacher on Maui by the name of Claudio. When he was present, the entire room settled into a magical place of peace. Jessica and I called him a tugboat. When you synced up with his energy field, he would pull you into the deepest waters of silence.

We can all get that tugboat effect with AWE as well, and can use it to counter the frantic, frenetic, freaked-out energy of the world around us. Whether it's a pandemic or global warming or a situation at work, AWE can help us stay centered through trying times and beyond.

The fact that you're reading this book means you're exceptionally energetically sensitive as you're drawn to this book and drawn to my work. I myself am exceptionally sensitive. I used to describe myself as a "skittish deer" because if something doesn't feel right, I'm out of there. I feel the energy of those around us, the energy of upcoming events, the energy of the land, and of course the energy of our kitty cats and our hyper-sensitive rooster Roo Roo.

I can feel what's going on with my clients well before they tell me, and I can feel what's going on with Jessica as well. Two empaths in a room can make for some challenging circumstances on occasion as our nonverbal feedback loops are through the roof. With that said, she is ten times more energetically sensitive than I, which makes it exceptionally important for her to be anchored in AWE, and to watch where and when she places herself to buffer the energy that's all around us.

Stop Repeating Patterns That Don't Serve You

It almost seems I was born into this world with an injury. From a forceps birth and temporary conehead, to cracking my head open three times by the age of two, to yearly accident after accident, even before my two near-death accidents and twin titanium femurs and hips—yup, I'm a tuning fork. It seems like I was incredibly accident prone.

While on Maui, after one last accident too many, one in which I fell on my bike, breaking all the ribs in front, behind, above and almost below my heart, I took inventory. I wanted to get to the bottom of this pattern and end the accidents, injuries, and way too much pain, in my opinion, before the next one. So I created a spreadsheet and documented thirty-six different incidents where I was breaking bones or being hospitalized.

I went into AWE and started asking about this pattern of injuries: "Where is this coming from?" "Why is this here?" "How is it here to serve me?" "How can I let it go?" And I heard something I'd heard once before in a past-life regression. It was that I had asked to get as many learnings or teachings this lifetime as I could, even though I knew that learnings often come with pain. I heard myself saying, "Give me the works!" In essence, I negotiated a soul contract that said I'd endure injury after injury so I could learn, so I could grow, and so I could use these teachings in order to help others.

Of course, once I understood this thoroughly, I asked in AWE if I could please renegotiate the contract. And between the past-life regression work, and my work in AWE, I'm finally, for the most part anyway, minus a broken toe here and there, completely injury-free.

You don't need to break bone after bone, or have injury after injury, in order for AWE to help you break patterns or renegotiate contracts.

If you have relationships that keep blowing up, or as my mentor Jack once told me, "I married the same woman three times," or if you keep finding yourself in dead-end job after dead-end job, you can bring that to AWE. You can bring just about any pattern you can think of, yes, certainly cycles of heartache, or addiction, or anything else you can think of.

We all have recurring patterns. But it's often hard to see our own blind spots. That's where AWE comes in, and even works as our own personal coach or counselor for that matter, because we can go into AWE and ask about our patterns: "Why do I keep repeating this relationship?" "Why do I keep getting the same dead-end job?" Or certainly, "Why do I keep hurting myself or getting sick?" Whatever it is, we can ask specifically about that in automatic writing.

Removing unwanted patterns is one of the most powerful ways AWE can help you. So when you see unwanted patterns, when you begin to recognize you're living the movie *Groundhog Day*, bring your patterns to AWE.

And you can do what I did as well: take inventory. Take inventory and look for repeated patterns. You can go into AWE and ask, "Do I have any repeating patterns?" You can write down a time line of your life and look for key events that stick out, and, of course, you can look for those repeating dwelling patterns in your mind. For your mind is your creator; wherever you put your attention is what you're going to create. So if you keep thinking, bad relationship, bad relationship, bad relationship, then, of course, relationship after relationship will end up on the rocks.

But AWE can help clear all of this.

It can help you find the patterns, see why the patterns are there, and, if you ask, even help you clear them. What does that mean? It means that we all hold energetic patterns in our field, whether you call that a magnetic field, your etheric DNA (I just made that up) or simply in the energy that is us, surrounds us, and binds us together— Dr. Ervin Laszlo, two-time Nobel Peace Prize nominee, even calls this the Akashic field. No matter what you call it, it's where we hold energetic wounds and traumas in our body. What are these? Well, if you find yourself repeating a pattern, or holding a grudge, or find that you overreact to different situations, or especially if you have PTSD, then you have an energetic pattern, wound, or block that gets to be cleared. Now there are dozens of modalities for doing so, from writing, to prayer, clearing statements, and more. And AWE can help you choose the modality that's best for your particular wound.

And if you need help, AWE may even suggest finding a coach, counselor, or energetic practitioner to help you clear them as well. Of course, two of my favorite techniques for clearing are EFT tapping (emotional freedom technique), which I teach and use with my clients and students, and *The Emotion Code* from Bradley Nelson, DC.

With EFT, you use clearing statements while tapping on one of eight or nine different acupressure points on the body to produce a parasympathetic nervous system response (this is a clinically proven technique particularly for severe wounds or trauma such as those among war veterans with PTSD).

The Dwelling/Antidote Exercise

We all have recurring patterns in our mind—what I call dwellings—where we're thinking about the same thought minute after minute, hour after hour, day after day. It's said we have 50,000 to 60,000 thoughts a day. I have no idea how anybody measures that. Do you click a button each time you have a thought? Click click click. Is it a spike on some sort of EEG?

But we know we keep thinking the same thought over and over again. Perhaps you're worried about the future, or kicking yourself about an event in the past, or maybe you think of yourself as an idiot for doing X or stupid for having Y or continuously worrying about your kids, finances, job, politics, health, or anything else you can think of (fill in your worry).

Here's a dwelling/antidote exercise to help you recognize these continuing thought patterns and let them go. Like taking a general inventory, in automatic writing, ask, "Angels, guides, light workers, or inner wisdom, what are the patterns that keep repeating in my mind throughout the day or that keep me stuck in my current ways?" Then write down whatever they tell you. This is a powerful way to recruit assistance and get answers.

I haven't defined them yet, but light workers are beings on the other side that are not angels. They could be a loved one, a friendly spirit, a pet that's passed on, anyone or anything who has a job on the other side for helping raise up humanity (you could even say they're your spirit team).

Take inventory. Get those thoughts all down in AWE before you ask for your single-minded purpose. Write your dwellings down in one column, and in a second column write down the antidote or the cure. What will counterbalance your repetitive thought or concern?

For instance, perhaps you're stuck watching and worrying about politics or simply the news. Write "focused on negative news" in one column, and in the second write an antidote: "whenever I focus on the news, I'll switch channels, or turn my mind to something positive I can do for myself or my family." In my case, when I found I was stuck on the news, I'd bring it back to working on this very book or planning an upcoming event. So the negative becomes a trigger for something quite positive.

For another example, if you find yourself calling yourself an idiot, you can write down on the dwellings side, "I call myself an idiot." Then you can say in automatic writing, "What would be a good antidote for this?" And maybe you hear, *Every time you call yourself an idiot, remind yourself of how loved and competent you are. Every time that you find yourself worried about finances, remind yourself of how capable you are and how well you've done at getting to this point.* Don't rely on your own answers. Instead recruit assistance and ask in AWE.

Put pen to paper and ask, "What is a good antidote to each one of the thoughts I dwell on?" Pick one or two major thoughts that consume you every day. What's the number-one concern you have? Tackle that one first.

If you chip away at this day after day, you'll find yourself getting lighter and feeling better, less stressed, and less on autopilot. You'll go from living reactively from your fear-based, dwelling monkey mind, to more proactive thinking. In essence, do this exercise, and you'll take back control of your mind and of your life.

For as Neville Goddard, and a more recent favorite author of mine, Mitch Horowitz, put it, your mind is creator. Truly, where you focus your mind is what you'll create. Or put another way, energy flows where attention goes. So do this exercise and put your attention, and creative energy, exactly where you want it.

Does This Serve Me?

We all make assumptions and filters in our minds, and we assume they are correct. For myself, I'm always thinking something's not in the fridge, because I don't expect it to be there. I'll literally look right past a giant jar of salsa, or bag of tortillas, because I don't believe it's there. Of course, when Jessica comes along, she doesn't have my assumption, or filter, and can spot the food item immediately.

AWE helps you see your blind spots, and move past your blind spots, or your filters. I am reminded of Einstein's adage that we can't solve a problem from the level from which it was created. AWE steps us back beyond our filters, beyond the information that we're allowing in, and gives us a set of eyes outside of ourselves.

We literally take in billions of bits of information a minute, but the brain can only process a few thousand—another one of those pieces of information I wonder how in the world was ever tested. But because of this, it means we can literally be blind to something right before our eyes.

Not only is this the case for salsa, tortillas, or even the oat milk, but it could be the case for a giant gorilla as well. An experiment conducted by Christopher Chabris and Daniel Simons in 1999 won the Nobel Prize. In the invisible gorilla experiment, test subjects were supposed to focus on counting how many times people pass a basketball. Because their minds were so focused on counting the passes, they completely missed the gorilla who walked in front of the passers right in the middle of the experiment.

It's a classic experiment (detailed in their book *The Invisible Gorilla*), which explains why we can't find the milk or the eyeglasses on our heads, the cell phone in our hands, or even the car keys that are right in front of us. It all goes to say that our mind literally plays tricks on us, as it filters out everything it assumes we don't need. But sometimes our assumptions are wrong.

We all make assumptions and have filters that keep us from being able to reach our highest potential, to achieve our greatness, to be able to discover who we truly are. For example, you may say you're not an artist. You might think you're not good at math. You could be concerned about whether you're doing your job at work well enough. You might think you're not spending enough time with family. You might be procrastinating about a home improvement project because you don't think you can do it well enough.

Whenever I say a statement like this, Jessica turns to me and looks me square in the eyes while saying "limiting belief." And she's right. Every one of these statements of what we can and can't do, can and can't be, or why that couldn't possibly be us is likely simply an assumption or belief that's stuck in your mind.

And while you might not be able to be a starting center in the NBA if you're 5 foot 1 and seventy-nine years old, even that belief gets to be challenged because you just never know.

The Open Box Exercise

What can we do to uncover who we truly are or to move past these assumptions and limiting beliefs? I call this the open box exercise. A simplistic explanation is this: I was searching for my ski boots in the garage. I searched everywhere. Seriously, everywhere.

It was the beginning of the new ski season, and I hadn't used the boots since the spring. I rearranged nearly every box and bin in the garage looking for the boots. I was quite thorough, because I knew if I asked Jessica, she'd ridicule me when she found them. She's a Scorpio and knows I can get lazy when looking and just ask her without looking, so she wants to make sure I do my due-diligence first.

And so I. Was. Thorough. Then when I absolutely exhausted everywhere I could think of (and that's the key, EVERYWHERE my mind, with my filters, could think of), when Jessica came home later that day, I asked if she knew where my boots were.

"Do you think they were stolen?" she asked.

I said, "Absolutely not. The odds are very good the ski boots are in the garage. I know they have to be here, there's simply some assumption in my mind that's blocking me from seeing them."

She marched into the garage intent on finding my boots. Within five minutes she pulled out a transparent plastic bin marked "plates and mugs," with the boots completely visible without even opening it up. Because I read "plates and mugs" on the bin, I couldn't see past the label. I couldn't see the gorilla because I wasn't looking for a gorilla.

What does that have to do with getting unstuck? It means if we really want to get unstuck, we need to be able to move past the labels and filters. We need to move past the assumptions about what's inside our boxes. How do we do this? Start taking inventory in AWE, again before you get to your SMP, of every assumption you have in your life.

Open up the boxes in your life—no matter what is on the label—and ask yourself, "Does this work? Does this not? Does automatic writing work?" I'd make a giant list of every possible assumption you can think of.

Jessica and I have started opening boxes recently. It's why we've begun changing the format of our *Inspire Nation* show, getting uncomfortable, and challenging ourselves in so many ways. We are literally opening each box of our lives and examining the contents.

"Does it feel good to be having four to five shows a week?" Open up that box, look at that assumption. "Hmmm, actually, we'd like to back off to two interviews and spend more time creating online courses." See how we moved past an assumption?

Then there's the hour-long format, the way we interview guests, even the green screen. Boy does Jessica hate the green screen. She's right, we get to challenge everything and take things to a new level.

By challenging everything in AWE, you can truly up-level and transform your life. Bring anything and everything to AWE. Don't be embarrassed—no one else has to read what you write, but bring it all, every habit, every pattern, almost every thought, Okay, that'd take a while. But in this way, you can bring automatic writing into everything: how you treat yourself, how you treat your kids, how you treat your partner, what you think about your job, what you think you're capable of, what you think you're not capable of, what your diet is, what your movement is, what your schedule is.

Look in every area of your life—friends, family, environment, time commitments, overall commitments, every area of your life—and bring that box of assumptions to AWE.

Opening the Box of Life

As I was writing this book, we were in the midst of COVID-19, and we just had our third miscarriage. The two events actually have a lot of similarities, for everyone. To me, the pandemic was like having a miscarriage. There were deaths of dreams, of hopes, of plans for the future. For many, all of our dreams, or how we thought life was *supposed to* go, went up in smoke as the world searched for normalcy.

So what do we do? For ourselves, it means questioning everything. Getting out of that box and asking what fits, what doesn't, or what needs to be changed or entirely thrown out. We've asked about our relationship, our home, our business, our stuff, our cars, our country, literally, just about everything—except for the kitty cats.

But when you're shaken by a "life-quake" to the core, it's important that you step back and ask the hard questions. Of course, we've done a lot of this work in AWE with our angels or guides acting as coach, helping us navigate this time to heal and to figure out where to go from here.

Everything's on the table, but with AWE we know we won't make rash decisions, but some very powerful ones to help us heal and move ahead. When we can let go of the grief, it's actually quite an exciting time. Out of AWE we keep hearing two powerful messages, both for ourselves and our clients.

1. **You're not allowed to know the answers now.** Meaning, this time of uncertainty, confusion, or chaos is to help serve us, and our only job is to work on ourselves, and how to step forward—this doesn't mean we can't serve others, but it means we can't try to figure it all out now. Consider the analogy or metaphor of a butterfly in a chrysalis, which really is us at this time. When the caterpillar's entombed in silk, it doesn't know what it will be when it comes out. And in the midst of the experience, it's literally digested itself with its enzymes, and while certain cells go where the eyes will be, the brain will be, and so forth, in the middle of the process, it's just a pile of primordial ooze. Which really is us right now, as a collective, and as individuals.

2. **If not now, then when?** AWE keeps challenging us to make great changes now. To go for things now. To get out of our box, now. If not now, then when, it keeps saying.

Use AWE to Make Better Decisions

Recently, Jessica and I went for our usual walk in town before sunset. As we were driving home, the clouds began to glow cherry red. We turned our brilliant yellow Tesla around and headed for the hills in hopes of catching a magical glimpse. Unfortunately, the colors faded as we made our way to the top of a hill.

I turned around, thinking everything in life happens for a reason, and soon enough, we found out why. They say, "Why did the chicken cross the road?" and to me, the answer to that's still uncertain. But in this case, coming down a country highway out of the hills, a rooster crossed the highway before me. It was near dark, windy, and cars were whizzing by.

I pulled off as safely as I could, and miracle of miracles, after walking and talking with the bird for a while, I was able to rescue it. But the rescue was the easy part; the harder part was what to do once getting it home (first live rooster in a Tesla perhaps)? And so what did I do? I went into AWE to ask how to care for this bird.

As crazy as it seems, AWE can answer almost any question, even how to care for and potty train a wayward rooster. His name is now Lucky Ruby Roo Roo, or Roo Roo for short, and according to AWE (and trusted animal communicators for confirmation), he's family and here to stay for life.

AWE is our decision-making tool of all tools. It can answer almost any question, or at least point you on your way. And not just for roosters. But for dilemmas, feeling stuck, or even knowing whether you're on track or off. Why? Because AWE takes you out of the thinking mind. As I mentioned earlier from Einstein, you can't solve a problem from the same level of energy from which it was created. Or put another way, imagine being stuck in a box with a piece of paper that says "instructions printed on the outside." It's not until we can get out side of our box of our lives that we've put ourselves in, that we can see what's going on and set ourselves free. And that's where AWE steps in, because it was never inside the box to begin with.

Of course, AWE can also give you wisdom beyond yourself— meaning from a higher place, a higher source, or even a higher being. The thinking mind, also called the small self, or your ego, always goes to a place of fear. It's actually trying to protect you. And to protect you, it will keep you in the smallest box it can, even if that actually hurts you.

Rather than other spiritual teachers who want you to shed the ego, move above the ego, or even eliminate or destroy the ego, I love the ego. I want to integrate the ego, make friends with the ego, and learn from my ego. But the ego is your wounded inner child that's going to act from a place of fear to keep you safe. If that means keeping you hiding under the bed where you lose your job, where you lose your income, where you lose your house, that's what your ego would do in a twisted way to protect you.

What does this mean? It means we get to rise above the worries of the ego by putting our questions to AWE.

I've had countless clients looking for new jobs or looking to make major shifts in their lives who've done so successfully by bringing their questions to AWE. And I'm talking the biggest of life decisions, whether dealing with death, divorce, audits, moves, you name it.

One way we can describe this is whether we are making decisions from a place of fear versus love. When we're problem-solving, brainstorming (isn't that an interesting word), or thinking of a solution, the fear-based ego kicks in, and we end up with fear-based answers. But when we bring our question to AWE, the guides don't have a dog in the fight, they're simply coming from a place of love, and so that's what you get, answers based in love.

The key point here is that this is really a decision about fear versus love or what feels light versus what feels heavy. In AWE you begin cultivating this discernment, shifting how you think about the decision-making process itself.

Rise Above the Fear

Before we bring a question to AWE, it's often confusing and flipped upside down and backward in the mind. Why is that? Because we've been trained that fear is bad. But fear is simply an emotion or energy in motion. Fear can be good or even great. When you're crossing the road (with or without a rooster), fear helps you to be cautious and could help you make better decisions to avoid oncoming traffic. In that sense, fear is good.

But all too often, fear causes us to hesitate, hold back, or even freeze up in the middle of traffic, and that's not good. There's a different way of viewing fear that you can cultivate through AWE and that can help you make better decisions, or learn there's a time and a place to actually lean into, or snuggle up with, your fear—a big shout out to Ram Dass for the use of the term snuggle up.

I like to call F.E.A.R., feeling excitement after realignment. So viewing fear in a different way—or viewed actually by flipping fear on its head, that's the realignment piece—fear is a powerful, potent, positive fuel. You're going to look both ways and you're going to move quickly and expeditiously to get across the road.

To me, fear and anxiety are excitement in disguise. Or fear and anxiety are excitement without deliberate motion. In other words, as a child, we were excited and went for things before we were told it was dangerous, or to be careful, or to watch out. Then we got confused. But that initial impetus for action that's what fear actually is and wow can it really help us, when we get it clear in our minds.

It doesn't mean that we shouldn't pay attention, be careful, or look before we leap, but we should make an honest assessment of what this fear is, where it came from, and how it is here to serve us.

Take for example a running race. If you've ever been at the starting line of a running race, or any other race for that matter, then you've felt the butterflies in your belly and that extreme sense of fear and adrenaline coursing through your veins. You are in fear. But then the moment the gun goes off, you feel much better. What happened? In essence, you had a wave of energy coursing through you waiting to help you with the run. Once you started stepping forward, the fear immediately transmuted into excitement and deliberate motion.

Talk about fear, our dear friend Carol said, "In November of 2018 I launched a podcast and a blog. I had left my corporate career of over two decades and suddenly was feeling major impostor syndrome. Who was I to start an online community? Who was I to cohost a podcast? Who was I to write a blog? All of these questions swirled in my head. Fear was beginning to take over. Had I made a terrible mistake? I turned to automatic writing as I often do in times of fear and uncertainty. The download? It was all about trust and how I'm supported at all times. They explained that I simply need to learn to receive. My higher team even mentioned Michael!"

A page from Carol's journal showing how AWE gave her answers and helped her make a major life decision.

The Power of Deliberate Action

I want to bring that phrase up again—*fear is excitement without deliberate action*—for this is a critically important concept.

When you're at the starting line of the race and you're in fear, once you start running forward, taking deliberate steps toward your goal (whatever your goal is, but in this case finishing the race), then you feel much better. Why? Because you're taking deliberate steps toward your goal.

But what if we mixed up two goals? What if you're at the starting line of a race and you pull out a journal to start writing a book. Chances are, you'll still be a mess, or worse, particularly if you then miss the start because you weren't paying attention. And if you're jittery about writing your book, and so instead you go for a run, you might burn off some nervous energy, but you'll still feel terrible about the book after the run.

Why? Because fear and anxiety are markers or pointers toward your goal. When you focus in on your goal, then the fear and anxiety are transmuted—that's the word deliberate for taking deliberate action. But if instead you simply burn off the energy by doing something else, then the fear stays with you, until you take deliberate action toward your goal.

So the most important question we could ask in AWE is this one: "Is this fear that's supposed to stop me in my tracks or is this excitement in disguise?"

Years ago, I was using AWE to help distinguish whether my fear of filming ten-minute videos for YouTube was excitement in disguise or actual fear from inner wounds. With AWE I asked: "What is this fear about?" And I was told it is excitement, about stepping forward, about reaching toward my dreams, and healing some wounds and blocks.

Whether you're exploring a period of reckoning, or healing old wounds, to looking at reinvention, or stepping forward into our future selves, AWE can help you heal and help you to molt, shedding the old skin, and step into the new. What a time to be alive, particularly when you have an inner GPS to help you step into your greatness, snuggle up with the fear, and lean into the new you.

What Fears Can You Address with AWE?

You can bring almost any fear or question you can think of to AWE. Just realize, in the beginning your egoic mind might have a tantrum, or fight back, but more on that in a moment.

So let me challenge you. Bring all your heavy, daunting questions to AWE like these:

- "Do I stay or do I go in this relationship?"
- "Do I stay or do I go in this job?"
- "What is going on with my child?"
- "I'm considering moving—is this right for us? Is this right now?"
- "What do I need to learn or know about this question and this decision?"

Bring all of your questions to AWE and ask. Don't think small. No question should be off-limits because, just like the open box exercise I introduced, you need to open every box in your life. When you bring the heavy decisions to AWE, you want to be completely open and honest and transparent and allow for your greatest dreams to take place, which may be even bigger than you have allowed yourself to dream.

And you want to bring your greatest fears, for truly, as Rumi the poet put it 800 years ago, the wounds are where the light shines through.

Most importantly, AWE won't let you play it small. None of us came here to play a small game, as we all came from the Divine, no matter how you define that. And so, AWE will call you on this. You may have had this pull to do something big, but you pulled back instead, you withdrew, grew small, and you said to yourself, "I can't possibly ask that." Or perhaps you said, "What, me? I couldn't possibly do that. Or I couldn't start that company or become that wealthy. Or even become famous. I'm not capable of that."

AWE will call you on this fast. For not once has AWE said to a single person, you're not destined for greatness or a great life, if you simply step into the fear, and step forward into your life.

Whatever decision you want to make, you deserve the greatest gifts in the world. You deserve the most amazing life. You are the most incredible, wonderful, over-the-top amazing human being, and you will have those results in life if you dare to put the pen to paper and ask those enormous questions. And then step forward. Life is a two-step dance: (A) ask, and be willing to listen and receive; (B) take action.

How Can I Use AWE to Make Positive Changes in My Life?

Building on the momentum of the previous question about using AWE to help make decisions, let's look at AWE in the sense of helping us make life changes, big and small.

Earlier I mentioned we're moving from a period of reckoning to reinvention. What does that mean? It means that we're often faced with a time of unprecedented challenges and changes, and certainly 2020 was such a time.

Spiritually, it's a time where everything that's been hidden under the carpet, such as our wounds, traumas, and habits from the past that no longer serve us, both individually and collectively, are coming up to be cleared and healed. And after they're cleared, something else gets to take its place. For once you clear the grooves in the record, you get to make new music.

So the question is, what gets to change? Or what doesn't need to change?

When "life-quakes" happen, we tend to ask ourselves what's going on, why can't I have things back to the way they were, and what in the world do I need to change to feel happy, stable, secure, or better about my life?

A couple key considerations. In AWE you can ask, "What gets to be changed in my life?" This is a powerful question. Or you can ask, "What's working for me and what's not?" Or one of my favorite questions: "Is there anything I'm missing or not seeing that needs to be changed?" In other words, "Automatic writing, please help me find what my blind spots are because my mirrors have fogged."

And then there's another all-time favorite question: "AWE, am I out of alignment?" This is such a biggie it cannot be overstated, as AWE can explain why you feel like water flowing uphill, or as if you're jamming the gears of life.

AWE repeatedly tells me that comfort is the enemy of greatness, and one could say that of our own personal evolution. I believe that's one key reason Mother Earth hit the red button or full stop on life in 2020 so we could reevaluate everything and make midstream course corrections—individually and collectively.

You can even ask if you are running on autopilot or have habits that no longer serve you. For it is only when we get off autopilot and off the highway and onto the twisty-turny mountain roads that we find a new way of being.

AWE can help you get out of the comfort zone and experience the world outside of your habitual and habituating patterns. This is where the juice is. This is where we're truly living. And in AWE, you'll be continuously challenged to get off autopilot and learn, grow, and expand. We're habituating beings. We want to do everything on autopilot, which means even when we ask ourselves what to do differently in life, we're going to get the same answers unless we start doing things differently.

Bring your questions, your habits, your life-long habituations back to AWE. You will get different answers or see a different way of living. Not more difficult, in fact, because going from Sisyphus pushing a stone uphill to getting in the flow could be much, much easier. But we get to change, and through this change we spirituality, emotionally, and perhaps even physically evolve.

That's why I'm always challenging people to go to the upper room (more on this later) and to vibrate at the highest level possible. It's not that AWE won't give you straight-shooting answers or give you a workable answer if you ask it at any time. It's that as you evolve, or vibrate at a higher level, you tend to get higher level answers. All answers are good answers, but AWE won't give you more than you can handle, to help you on your way.

As one AWE practitioner, Betsy, told me,

> I began taking the AWE course when I was working on many things in my life. I was working on developing my psychic-mediumship abilities while also trying to be happy with myself. I began the course with trying to connect with my higher self or my subconscious. At first, I really didn't know

what would happen, but I found that I could just write the questions to which I was seeking answers over and over and then some expression, song lyric or just a few simple words would appear and really just boil the whole issue down for me. I have always been a doer, which means I can constantly be doing things without feeling accomplished or satisfied. My automatic writing kept bringing me answers like *slow down, one step at time, you are enough,* and, *just listening does more for your kids than all of your doing.* I found this very comforting and extremely helpful.

When you're stuck on the couch, when you're not moving forward, when that energy is not circulating through you because you're not figuratively driving down different streets, AWE is going to give you tiny steps forward. If you're challenging yourself, if you're getting out of your comfort zone, if you're doing something different each and every day, you're energized, and AWE will give you more powerful answers to help you on your way.

As I like to state with AWE, "Please give me answers for my highest good and the highest good of all." When you're at a lower vibrational state versus a higher vibrational state, you need a different answer, not a better answer to help you move ahead. The key word is *different,* for there's no judgment on the path, and there's no one person or one state better than another, simply different.

You are where you are, until you're not. That's called stepping forward, and AWE will help you do just that.

If you're stuck, simply take tiny steps forward to help get the energy flowing. Of course, when a client is stuck, I encourage them to go to AWE. It's a loving, kind, nonjudgmental voice that will give them the absolute best first step to take. When we're talking about getting unstuck, we're talking about how much we can get that energy flowing.

Each and every day, try something different and then bring it back to AWE. Ask: "Why am I stuck?" "What's the meaning behind this?" and "What's the best first step I can take?"

If I've learned anything from AWE, it's that micro-gains over a massive period of time surpass massive heroic leaps any day. Why? Because micro-gains have stickiness, they have habituation, they have permanence. Do some each morning, like AWE for twenty to thirty minutes for a month or two, and you have new neural pathways, a myelinated superhighway in your brain, or deep grooves that make it easy to go on autopilot and keep doing your AWE.

Conversely, writing in AWE two days in a row, or even for an entire weekend, and just writing and writing might yield some interesting results, but there's no way to make a habit without consistency. Even more so, when we are doing something on willpower versus autopilot, we burn out, stop what we're doing, and are likely never to do it again.

So gauge success in the micro-gains. You can climb the mountain, but take one tiny step forward each day. Do the same tomorrow and the day after. Be like Mother Nature, with a drop of rain creating the Grand Canyon over an eon. You will create almost anything you desire by making little changes methodically each and every day.

How Jessica and I built our podcast empire may be a useful example of sticking with micro-gains here. When we first started our *Inspire Nation* show, we were complete and total unknowns in the podcast world. Even getting a guest on the show took twenty emails, a lot of coaxing, or more. Had we tried to do everything at once—emails, booking guests, prep, recording, editing, posting—we would have completely burned out, and, poof, like so many other podcast start-ups, we'd be gone.

Instead we took a slow and steady approach, chipping away at the giant mountain. We got organized, got systems in place, and ever so slowly but steadily built a sustainable business that has turned into an empire. Just as the expression goes, slow and steady wins the race, or as AWE recommends and we put on the back cover of our Barefoot Running book, take a "go slow to go fast" approach. Then build your empire.

Get Moving—as in Exercise

What in the world does movement have to do with AWE and getting unstuck? Well, apparently, everything.

When we're stuck, what we're really saying is our energy isn't cycling through us, it isn't moving. The energy is pooling, which literally can lead to illness, injury, and disease. What does this mean?

First, we can go into AWE and ask, "How do I get physically moving? How do I get this energy moving?" In other words, "How do I get back into flow?" Then challenge yourself to move more.

Now you're probably wondering why I'm talking about movement when the AWE process involves quiet meditation and writing. But I am suggesting that you do five to thirty minutes of movement after you do your automatic writing before you go about your day.

Why would I suggest that? One of the ways that spiritual people get confused is that they don't play the game at the physical level. They believe, "I'm spiritual. I'll play it up here in the ether. I'll play it up in alchemy. I'll play it with the law of attraction. Or even by opening my chakras, a kundalini experience, or by playing the enlightenment game."

All of that is fine, but we came here incarnate, in flesh, in form, in this physical suit, a meat suit, a rental suit, if you will, so that we could learn how to move and play on the physical plane, which means we need to address the energy, the chi that is moving through our physical bodies.

Physical movement affects the mind, the heart, every part of the physical body, and movement certainly affects your ability to get unstuck.

I'm not suggesting a workout fit for someone competing on American Ninja. Not at all. I'm suggesting a walk. Spend time in nature.

Interestingly enough, after you've been practicing AWE and connecting with that voice, you'll begin to hear it and feel it more and more, beginning with time in nature. It's during those quiet walks, especially in nature, the voice of AWE begins to get louder and louder—perhaps because everything else is quieter.

Yes, you could do a treadmill or your stair stepper, but I encourage you to actually build distance in nature or across terrain in whatever you're doing. Do movement that promotes distance. Why? Because it takes you further away from your mind, from your thoughts, from your problems, and from being stuck.

What other movement? Tai chi is amazing. Qigong is phenomenal. There are so many different exercises to get energy flowing.

What if you could get up right now and go walk outside for five or ten minutes? When I am working on interviews and I am feeling stuck, I will literally throw myself out the door, walk a hundred yards downhill down the driveway, turn around and go, "Oh, my God, that's a big hill," and turn around and come a hundred yards back. I find I am no longer stuck. Energy is flowing.

At work, can you go up and down some stairs? Walk to the bathroom on another floor? Go to your car in the parking lot and back? Take a stroll around a retail store or mall? Find the places and time to get unstuck with movement to get your energy flowing.

Organize and Plan Your Day with AWE as Your Personal Assistant

One of the double-edged swords about automatic writing is that if you're too awake, you don't get deep words of wisdom. Instead, you get a to-do list for the day. While on the surface this sounds like a bad thing, you can actually use it to your advantage.

Just imagine if you had a magical personal assistant you could call on anytime, like a Siri from the beyond? Well, with AWE you do. When you finish your automatic writing, or even later in the day if you go back into AWE, you can ask for help in organizing your day.

It's especially powerful first thing in your day, to set you up for the kindest, gentlest day, the one that's highly focused and incredibly in the flow. After you ask "What's my SMP?" you can literally dive in and ask about your day: "What do I do first?" "What needs to get done?" "What's the order I do things in?"

You could, literally, crack open your calendar and go through hour by hour or almost minute-by-minute while you're still in the automatic writing space and schedule your day.

At this time you're thinking most clearly or you're plugged in most powerfully, and you're able to know what to do and when. AWE can be a tremendous help with prioritizing. That's something that I've been challenged with in the past, weighing my priorities.

When you go into the automatic writing state, your vision for the day becomes much clearer and easier to move tasks around in your calendar. AWE will help you with planning and prioritizing and even help with daily reminders (especially important for me).

You can also come back to AWE any time later in the day. Let's say you're stuck, or confused, or overwhelmed, as we all can be. Or even more critically, perhaps you have conflicting priorities later in the day. Simply put on your theta music, go quiet for a minute, write out your prayers, and ask, "What do I need to know for the rest of the day?" or "How do I handle these conflicting demands?" or "What do I do and in what order for the rest of the day?" Or most importantly, "What's the one most important task I get done this afternoon, or before I wrap things up?"

While AWE can't necessarily give you more hours in your day, it can help you get more done, with less pressure, and feel better about yourself or be kinder to yourself in the process. It's the kind-gentle-easy executive assistant that's always there if you need it, and always on your side.

* * *

While it's so easy to be overwhelmed and frozen with fear, AWE can help you get unstuck. It's done that time and time again for Jessica and me. With AWE we've found a way to restart the engine metaphorically, get the energy flowing, and get moving in a positive direction with our lives, our show, our business, and our finances.

I've never found a single client who couldn't rediscover powerful forward momentum and positive life direction when they began practicing automatic writing. If anything, they got so excited they'd almost want to do too much at once. Of course, that's where AWE comes to the rescue by helping them figure out what to do when, and in what order, for a kind-gentle-easy up-leveling of their lives. And, boy, does that process transform their energy!

11 | Raise Your Vibration with the Automatic Writing Experience

Even if you haven't channeled any profound words of wisdom yet, chances are you will still feel a lightness about you with the practice of automatic writing. This is the hidden benefit of automatic writing attunement.

The Pledge—
Going to the Upper Room

Imagine viewing life from a higher perspective, a higher vantage point, or a higher level of energy from which you're operating from pure love and no judgment. AWE can help get you there. Not overnight, of course, but day by day, because each time you go into AWE, you're raising your vibration to the upper room.

I first heard about going to the upper room from Paul Selig, author of *I Am the Word, Beyond the Known: Realization* and *Alchemy: A Channeled Text*, and from his guides, and then it started coming through in automatic writing day after day. With guidance, I've been able to go to the upper room and stay there more often, or stay in a higher state of beingness.

What does this require? A commitment to a different way of viewing the world and transforming the energy we see.

As an alchemist, I'm continuously transforming the energy all around me. To me, that's what it means to go to the upper room, transforming the lower-level vibration or energy you see all around you to a higher state. And this brings you up as well.

It all begins with a commitment, and a simple way to make this commitment to a higher way of being is through a basic pledge. For words have energy, and spoken words have a powerful effect on the Universe. Even more powerful are written words for they are literally taking energy (ideas) and transforming them into matter (words on a page). As they say, energy flows where attention goes. When you write a commitment, rather than simply saying it in your head, you cause tumblers to fall into place and begin to transform your entire outer existence.

Your mind is a creator, and when you write these words, you take a powerful step toward creating a new, higher-vibrational state of reality.

The Pledge

Please write this down word for word or modify as you see fit. But make sure you write this:

> I, [*your name*], pledge to always look for the best in each and
> every situation, and in each and every one, especially starting
> with myself. I come from love, I am love, and I will choose to
> look at the world from a lens of love, each and every chance I
> can. I commit to choosing the upper room, to filling myself

with love, and to vibrating at the highest level possible. I am
free. I am free. I am free. Thank you. Thank you. Thank you.

Yes, this does mean choosing love over fear. This does mean looking at the world differently and doing your best to recognize that
everyone is your brother, mother, sister, father. It means starting to
look at each situation as to how this can serve you rather than to question why something is happening.

With this pledge, you choose to go to the upper room. You're setting an intention to raise your vibration every day. You realize negativity in the mind is contagious. I call this the negativity flu, spreading
not only from one person to another but from one cell to the next and
to the next, or from one thought to the next to the next.

Of course, you can spread a virus of positivity as well. For when
you choose the upper room, and when you dive into AWE, your positive energy becomes contagious.

I hear a Native American parable time and time again, and it still
bears repeating: A grandfather tells his grandson that there are two
wolves on his shoulders. On one shoulder there's a good wolf, on the
other a bad wolf. And he shares, they're constantly in battle.

The child asks his grandfather, "Grandfather, which wolf will
win?"

The grandfather responds, "The one you feed."

This is such a key point, for when you make a commitment and
go into AWE daily, you're transformed, you're uplifted, and you are
feeding the good wolf.

If, instead, we stop going into AWE, we focus on the negativity or
get stuck in the N.E.W.S. (negative worthless stimulation), if we feed
the negativity of our minds, we lower our vibration and the world
around us changes. What we see is different, the situations we attract

are different, even the people we attract into our lives are different depending on whether we commit to the good wolf or the bad.

It's not that we attract badness into our lives, but we can only see at the level we're vibrating. And so life becomes no fun, at least temporarily. When we feed the bad wolf, it's hard to hear the words of AWE or take action on them. On the other hand, when we feed the good wolf, everything in our lives can change.

So what does this mean? If you catch yourself focused on the negative, thinking negatively, or in a place of gloom and doom—not to mention doomscrolling, a surefire way to pull you into the gutter— then it's time to bring things to AWE. (*Doomscrolling* is continuing to surf or scroll bad news even when it makes you feel sad and depressed.)

Ask what's going on, why you're feeding the bad wolf, and what you can do to bring yourself out of a funk. Often we're addicted to the negative. Rick Hanson, author of *Hardwiring Happiness*, said our brains were designed to look for danger, to look for the tiger that's about to pounce. It's literally hardwired into our DNA to keep us safe. The trouble is, the brain will always find danger, and so it's always on a heightened state of alert and always wants to swim in the sewer—in essence to keep us safe.

So when you bring your negativity to AWE, what you're really asking is help with letting go of the negativity and learning how to rewire for the positive.

In your automatic writing, ask for help in finding your blind spots and viruses hiding with the negativity flu and see how you can ferret them out. Sometimes you can get rid of negativity by not eating bad foods. Avoid too much TV news. Choose not to listen to the negativity of others. Spend less time on mindless social media.

You can either raise yourself up to the higher room or let negativity bring you down. And maybe the next time you watch the news, you ask yourself how it makes you feel. An oh-I-feel-great sense? Inspired? Or dragged down in the muck?

Choose to go to the higher room. Take the pledge. And ask in AWE what habits you can dump that are bringing you down. (This may also be a good time to revisit the Ego Dump exercise in chapter 3.)

Heal Deeply Rooted Emotional Wounds

Daily negative assaults, as just described, are one thing. But healing deeply rooted emotional wounds is quite another. You know what these wounds are. They rock you to the core.

Let's say, for instance, you have an argument with a spouse, with a partner, with somebody in your life and you lose your cool and you don't understand why something so small can end up having such a wounding emotional reaction.

Or you keep losing job after job. Or maybe it's overreacting each time someone is late, or you find you can't ever get yourself someplace on time. Maybe you feel everyone is belittling you. You take criticism too personally. These patterns just keep coming around and around, until the wound is cleared.

For myself, it used to be feeling like I made a poor decision, no matter what I did. And for Jessica it was feeling as if she wasn't being heard. We all have these wounds.

Another example would be people who keep inviting "energy vampires," as Christiane Northrup, MD, likes to call them, into their lives. Whether it's poor dating experiences, a particularly bad boss, or anyone else who has a toxic influence on you, no matter what you do, these people who suck your energy keep finding you—until you can get the energetic wounds routed out and cleared.

We all have triggers (and the triggers, although now weaker with AWE, don't go away; they're here for us to learn), but with AWE, they no longer hold us hostage.

As another powerful example from AWE, for me, just thinking about going live on YouTube used to freeze me up because of some deep rooted wound inside me that hadn't been addressed. As I approach these situations I would say to myself, "It's okay. You're safe. Let's bring it to AWE. Why am I feeling this way? What's going on? Where are these triggers coming from?"

Then I address the situation in AWE. I write about it and be honest with what takes place. Now I rock the YouTube live events. AWE helped me completely reverse my fear. Now, even when I haven't prepared properly, I surrender into AWE and the words come.

So for that person you're really upset with and don't know why, don't be embarrassed or ashamed. Take it to AWE and say, "Why am I so triggered by this person? What does it mean? What can I learn from this person or this situation? Or as I like to say, why are they my teacher now?" Get to the root of it. It's important that you ask the deepest questions. You can then ask if there are any thought exercises, writing exercises, or other practices that can get at these wounds. Pull on the golden thread of these wounds and get to the end of it so that you can set yourself free.

While I was working with AWE on recovering from my fear of screwing up, like with my on-air interviews, AWE gave me a basic mantra. You can use mine as well, but you can also ask in AWE for your own personal mantra. Never mind having to pay hundreds of dollars to a guru. Here is my mantra: "I am good. I am great. I am kind."

And so what I say to myself in the evening, when my mind wants to freak out and tell me all the things that I haven't gotten done, I simply repeat, "I am good. I am great. I am kind. I am good. I am great. I am kind. I am good. I am great. I am kind."

When I repeat my self-affirming mantra, it's like I'm giving myself a big hug or a heart massage. I feel better if I can remember to do it when going to sleep because I wake up more rested as well. And once you discover what your wound is (if you don't know, ask in AWE), then ask this: "What do I do to clear this?"

Other techniques such as EFT tapping, Emotion Code, or shamanic journeying through drumming can address deep-seated wounds as well, but those practices are beyond the scope of this book. Whether you address your wounds with AWE or with other methods, I'm talking about moving past these energetic blocks and wounds, healing your subconscious, and shorting out parts of our subconscious, and shorting out the negativity.

One practitioner of AWE, Tina, shared an intensely personal story. Here are her words:

> I discovered automatic writing quite by accident after my husband died. While deep in my grief, I began writing about my despair as a way of purging my anguish. My journaling turned into poetry writing and the most profound words of wisdom spilled out onto the pages of my journal. Things that didn't sound like myself spilled out like beautiful medicine for my soul. I have dozens and dozens of Dollar Store composition books that I use for my journaling.
>
> Creating a sacred space for doing my automatic writing is so important to me. I chose a beautiful area near an outside

window with a view to the nature preserve in my yard. Over time and with consistency, this became my sacred space used specifically for my conversations with Spirit. Now I experience a heightened awareness as I enter this space; I immediately sense my guides/Spirit/the Divine. I begin to get a buzzing sensation like a frequency through my ear chakras as the words begin to flow.

Actually, when this first happened to me when I was journaling my grief, I thought something was wrong with my ears. So I went to the doctor just to be sure I didn't have tinnitus. The intensity was so strong it was almost painful. Once I confirmed that nothing was "wrong" with me physically, I realized I was having a spiritual transformation, and the intensity settled down (I understand now that it was fear that made it painful). I thought I was "broken," but I came to understand that, instead, I was BROKEN OPEN.

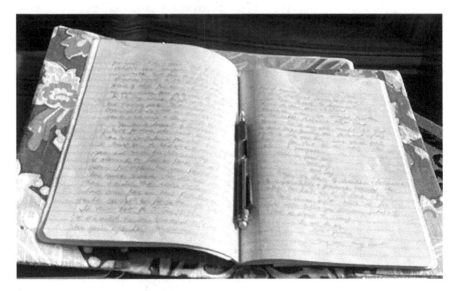

Tina's journal pages and her profound insight.

Overcome Fear and Anxiety

When you can't please everyone, your nervous system goes into overdrive. There's fight, flight, freeze, and freak out. And when you can't please everyone, and it's tearing you apart, that's where you freak out. So what does freak out have to do with AWE?

Humanity, for example, was in a global freak-out during the start of COVID-19. I personally am not viewing that time as a gloom and doom period. In fact, I believe that collective life-quake was necessary to shake loose the shackles of the old and make way for the new. Nothing we're doing or have done as of late is sustainable. In essence, we've reached the end of an epoch, the end of living from greed and corruption, and stripping the earth of her resources. Mother Earth has hit the giant red reset button. And as I've learned through AWE, we can learn and make change the easy way or the hard way. And so often we choose the latter.

When you are torn in your decisions, bring your emotions to AWE. Share, open up, be honest, or simply have the courage—I'm by your side rooting you on—to ask for help in AWE. AWE can help you see the big picture, sort through the mess, and keep you from tearing yourself apart. Oh I pray for the day our leaders will learn about AWE, for when you plug into the Divine, things become much clearer and we begin to act with greater kindness and compassion.

So when you're feeling worried, stressed, anxious, torn apart, or depressed, bring it to AWE. Ask "What's going on?" "Where's this coming from?" "How is this here to serve me?" and most importantly, ask how you can heal this wound, or this pain, and move beyond it, or at least temper it.

For myself, it's that pesky "screw up" gene. When it flares up and I feel the fear, I need to go to AWE to get realigned. "What's going on here?" I'll ask. "Haven't I taken care of this?" But, alas, some wounds are here to guide us for a lifetime, or so it appears, but they can grow fainter and fainter. So I bring my wounds to AWE, and it tells me what to do and how to heal, especially when you hit that good ol' surrender button I mentioned earlier and bring it to AWE.

Sometimes AWE will give me a mantra, or a simple way to reframe my fear. Or a bigger picture perspective of everything that is going on. And that bigger picture perspective is often all I need to get out of a place of panic or fear and to see the bright side again. Or at least know that the world or our lives will be all right.

What are you waiting for?

In a Moment of Panic

Though it's the hardest thing in the world when your mind is going loopy, if you can get yourself to your headphones and your journal and go into AWE, you will feel so much better. For AWE can quickly calm you down, give you a bigger picture perspective, and help you see beyond your nervous system and your worried or freaked-out mind.

I can't say this is easy. When we're hyped up and our nervous system's on overdrive, it's often the last thing in the world you want to do. But if you can set yourself down in the chair and get yourself to write, it's like you're suddenly surrounded by angels, which you are, and everything starts to become clearer and you feel much better. And if you're being forced to make an important decision right there in the moment—and again, I'm Mr. Go Slow about these things, so take it as slow as you can—you can get guidance from a higher plane about what in the world to do and catch your breath before you do it.

Throw Off the Cloak of Depression

When I first started researching AWE, I had no idea how powerful the technique was in the psychology field dating back to the time of Jung and Freud. It was considered incredibly powerful more than 150 years ago for understanding the subconscious mind and healing wounds, anxiety, and depression.

I'm not a psychiatrist or a psychologist, but I have seen miracles happen through AWE. First, I've seen the most anxious, high-strung individuals finally feel safe and secure enough to let their guards down and melt into life. They were completely transformed.

When it comes to depression, I've seen spectacular results. While I don't call myself a channel or a medium, though perhaps that's an apt description, though not like a true savant, I can see a dark cloak around those who are depressed. And when that person goes into automatic writing, I see the cloak begin to fade away. It's as if with each session the cloak gets lighter and lighter, until it's fully gone. It's not that one specific thing was said in AWE that made all the difference. I believe it's the vibrational alignment or attunement with something greater than themselves that helped raise their vibration.

And it's given each of them hope and a new perspective. That's priceless. So if you're struggling or challenged with depression (I'd use the word *battling*, but I truly believe what we resist persists and what we fight against we only affirm and make stronger), so if you're challenged with depression and you bring it to AWE, even if you don't suddenly get the most profound words from the heavens itself, if you keep with it for even a few short weeks, you'll find you're feeling better. What have you got to lose—that old cloak? It doesn't suit you or fit you anyway.

12 | Manifest and Attract What You Desire through Automatic Writing

Writing in AWE is the perfect way to attract your future to you, that boldest, brightest future, that you can barely even imagine or dare to dream.

You can call in your future in many ways—I like to say that the future's already here, I call it the future-present. To me, one of the most amazing ways to call in this future is by writing a letter to yourself in AWE. But this is no ordinary letter, it's filled with energy and power, and, most importantly, it's not coming from you.

Just as we can call in angels, guides, and even deceased loved ones for wisdom and guidance, we can call in your future self as well.

"Hello, Me"—A Letter from Your Future You

Writing a letter from your future self could literally help you bypass or jump across subconscious blocks. It helps you attract things into your future, and it helps you understand from the future what is—what I like to call—a kind, gentle, easy, good path for you to take to get there.

Who's your future self? It's the you, or the me, that already exists five, ten, or even twenty years down the road.

Einstein proved that time isn't real, and certainly isn't linear, something that Einstein explained with $E = mc^2$. Basically, time is happening simultaneously everywhere. All time is happening at the same time. What this means is that your future is not set in stone. There are a multiverse of possibilities. But it means that your future self already exists and knows things about you that you couldn't possibly know.

Meanwhile modern experiments by researchers such as Dean Radin, PhD, indicate that the arrow of time is more flexible than it seems, and that we can literally tap into future possibilities with our minds. Experiments in precognition or the ability to know the future before it has taken place have been statistically demonstrated to six-sigma and beyond (according to MIT, six-sigma signifies experimental results that are better than a one-in-a-half-billion chance).

So what does this mean? It means, scientifically speaking, we can get in touch with our future selves, and in AWE we can literally write to our future and ask questions. You can ask your future self anything you want.

Now I believe gut feelings are connected to the angels and guides, but also to our future self. For when you ask a question and immediately feel a twinge, pain, or even punch in the gut, I feel it's your future self literally giving you a nudge to wake you up. Of course, your future self can also help you feel elated and on fire as well. Or as Jessica says, "Let's do this!" That's her future self giving her the greatest energy in the world.

So we can ask questions, we can get guidance, and we can even have your future self paint a picture of where you want to go and how in the world to get there.

That's where this exercise—truly one of my favorites—comes in. You can write a letter in AWE from, not to, your future self. You can choose any time period you want.

This exercise has proven time and time again, to be incredibly helpful, especially in overcoming subconscious blocks. So when I'm working with a coaching client, if we're trying to attract something in the immediate future, I might go to their one-year-from-now self and prompt them to write from that perspective. If we're trying to attract something that's kind of a medium distance away, I'll go to their five-year-from-now self. And then, obviously, if we're looking at a bigger picture, I may go ten or even twenty years in the future.

Doing so helps you leap past your subconscious wounds, blocks, walls, or blackouts (black holes that prevent you from stepping ahead) that are keeping you from stepping into your greatest, most amazing future possible.

Here's how to manifest using AWE. Simply put, you want to write something like this: "Hi, future self [or something to the equivalent]. Hi, future Michael. Or hi, ten-year-from-now Michael. What can you tell me about the future and what do I need to know now?"

And then you're off to the races—just as you do in AWE when you're asking yourself the question, "What do I need to know today?"—except you're asking your future self specifically to guide your present self. Let that wiser, more experienced version of you write and share whatever they want and feel free to ask questions.

And this future self can help, basically, grab that golden thread and pull you forward into your future, particularly bypassing the blocks that say, "I can't do this. I wouldn't know where to start. My perfectionism is keeping me frozen in place. I've got a wall that is preventing me from moving ahead."

Instead, your future self is saying, "Hello! I'm here. I've already seen how you do it. I've already seen what the pitfalls were, how you worked past them, how you got here. Would you like me to make it easier for you?"

Here's an example of a letter from my future self that I received in AWE:

Dear Michael,

I love you dearly, more than you could ever know. I'm so sorry you struggled so much in your early years. I know how hard that must have been for you. And the accidents, I'm so, so sorry you endured so much pain. But rest assured, you are on path, exactly where you're supposed to be.

As for the future, keep focusing on the books, on the show, and allow the future to unfold. You'll be moving, I know you don't want to hear that, but it's coming for you.

You are right, books are in your future, more than you could ever imagine, with a far greater reach than you could ever imagine. Keep this as your north star, you are a writer first and foremost, yes, after being a husband and a father, you do have 2 beautiful kids, not to worry, they are on their way.

But your job now is to hold space, to lean forward into the fear, and to allow beyond anything which you've ever allowed before. Don't try to make things difficult or complicated, even though that's your nature. Seek to simplify, to get light, and where you feel fear, keep challenging yourself. Your job at a deep core level is to lean into that fear, for it is a portal, a gateway, to something far greater than you could imagine. You are right, fear is excitement in disguise, but it is more than that, it's a gateway, a portal, a tunnel to greatness, or toward this current, present future self. And so I would encourage you, when you feel fear, when you feel a desire to recoil, to pull back, or even to run or yell, to instead perceive it with an inspector's eye. Get out your magnifying glass, say "Isn't that interesting?" and inspect it with everything you have.

You will often find that hidden inside that lump of coal is a diamond waiting to be discovered, dear one. It simply takes being present, leaning in, and yes, you love to say "snuggle up with fear" as Ram Dass used to say.

Explore like the world has been birthed anew and you're seeing everything for the first time. And challenge yourself in each and every way. Yes, of course, kind and gentle, but don't use that as an excuse to stay comfortable. For comfort truly is the enemy of greatness, and when you put yourself out there, you will find a Michael, stronger, more confident, more capable, and more self-assured than you ever imagined possible.

I send you so much love, dear one, I am here for you any time you need me. I am not just your future self, but I am you, I am family, I am *ohana*, and I am a guiding light and spirit within you. I am a diamond in the coal, and I can be recognized and called upon any time you wish.

I send you so much love, and can't wait to "see" you in the future. But of course, I already do see you, I am already here, and your future is so incredibly bright, yes, as the song goes, you gotta wear shades!

One of the outcomes I love so much about writing to, through, and especially from your future self is you can see yourself from the other side. And specifically I mean the other side of your subconscious blocks.

One of the most powerful ways I help clients move past a block, whether it be in work, or income, or relationships, is to write from their future self. Because the future self is already there, already on the other side, and has already found a way over, under, around, or through the block that is holding you back.

Your future self not only can give you the direction to overcome the block, but can put you in a state of vibration and knowingness that the block is no longer there. Once you are in this energetic state—writing from your future self where that block is gone—then the block no longer exists, even in the here and now. It's an incredibly powerful tool to help you move ahead.

Of course, writing to, through, or from your future self can help you manifest or attract into your life what you desire—if it's truly important to you. For your future self can help you see what's for your highest good, and what's not. And if it is for your highest good, your future self can help you bring it into reality.

Writing to your future self can help you move past this fear of the future, fear of stepping forward, and even the fear of the unknown. Your future self can give you a road map to the future and give you a taste of what it's already like.

Why would one be scared of a brilliant possible future—there are countless potential futures out there, a topic for another book, but when you tap into your future self, you are presented the most beautiful future possible. Why would you be scared of this brilliant future, if you could already see it, feel it, and have discussions with the you that's already living it?

When in doubt, when you want to attract, when you want to discover the greatness that you are and that you will be, write to your future self. Say, "Hello, me."

Automatic Writing for Dreaming Big

I've discussed sleep in an earlier chapter, and I hope you are using AWE to get a better, more refreshing night's sleep. But what about dreams or creating castles in the sky? Yes, AWE plays a role in daydreams and nighttime dreaming too. And they're closely interrelated. For energy flows where attention goes, and if you can focus on your dreams while you sleep, you can literally dream your future into reality. You can use automatic writing as a dream creation device.

I recommend doing this through a dream journal. Now, what's a dream journal? Some people write down their dreams, and that's actually something I'll talk about later. But, in this case, it's to help your subconscious to program your life. A dream journal is writing out what you want at night before going to sleep, to help you bring it about.

When you use automatic writing just before going to bed, you help set yourself up for beautiful dreams in the evening and for your subconscious to work on whatever it's been given. Actually, whether or not you do automatic writing, your subconscious will always be working in the evening on the last thoughts you give it.

If you're watching the news with gloom and doom, your subconscious is going to be working on gloom and doom throughout your sleep. If you've been watching horror movies about the latest zombies, then your subconscious will be focusing on zombies while you sleep. If you've been checking on your finances, there you are dreaming about money—or perhaps a lack thereof. And if you've been writing about your hopes, dreams and goals for the future, your subconscious is going to be trying to figure out all night long how to get that for you as well.

That's why dream journaling in automatic writing can be such a fantastic technique.

Now I'm not talking about simply going into automatic writing and saying, "I want a million dollars" or "I want a Lamborghini (electric anyone?)." I'm talking about writing down your dreams with more emotion, excitement, and energy for the future than you've ever mustered before. No, I'm not saying you have to dance around and put your hands up in the air and go, "Yes! I've got this!" though that couldn't hurt. But I'm talking about putting yourself in the emotional state of already having your dreams—and big, scary amazing dreams for that matter.

When you're writing in AWE to program your subconscious, give it everything you've got. Dream big and bright. When you write from this place, your subconscious goes to work on it all night long and tries to figure out how to make it your new reality.

The Bible stated 2,000 years ago, in Matthew 6:5-13, a key tenet of hermeticism, "as above, so below." What that means is this world is a mirror, a reflection of what's going on, on the other side, or as I like to say, beyond the veil. Therefore, if you go to sleep thinking about a new, exciting job, and you wake up thinking about a new, exciting job, then somewhere up above or on the other side of the veil, you are bringing a new, exciting job into your life.

One note: Do not think small or play it small for this exercise. The Universe doesn't like a small game, and you didn't come here to play it small or play it safe. Why? Because none of us are getting out of here alive, so we might as well make the most of it.

So what's that mean? If you want a better job, what's the scariest, most audacious, most out there job you can think of that you could possibly even remotely think of qualifying for? If you want to create a podcast, what's the most outrageous, world-renowned podcast possibility of a show you could ever think of creating? If you want to be well known, how famous could you possibly be? Or if you want a family, how much can you envision being the von Trapps, traveling the world, singing from the mountain tops?

If you can see it, feel it, and dream it, you can realize it.

Write out the boldest, most audacious dreams you can possibly imagine. They don't have to be directly linked to reality. If you want to fly like a bird, go for it. Your dreams don't have to be the types of thoughts that cause you to say, "I can definitely figure out how to get there."

These dreams can be your reach dreams, your dreams that are so audacious, like "in this lifetime I'd like to do an eco tour to the moon." Write that dream down on paper. Whatever it is, get it down, and then ask yourself: "What's the essence of what I'm dreaming about?"

For instance, if you're asking for a million dollars, and everybody wants a million dollars, ask: "Why do I want a million dollars?" Well, it could be the freedom that you get from having no financial worries. It could be the feeling of accomplishment or the ability to use that money to help others or the ability to use that money to help your kids or that money gives you the opportunity to get some help on board so that you have more time in your day. That's the essence.

Then write down the essence, the emotion, and what's behind that emotion. Feel it before you sleep. Imagine being there, feeling it, living it, doing it. Boy, would bouncing up and down on the moon and driving one of those rovers feel fun.

Do this exercise before you go to bed with automatic writing. Set your intention. Your subconscious will be working on that throughout the entire time you sleep and beyond.

Reprogram Your Subconscious with AWE

Hopes, dreams, setting your intention—all are part of the beauty inside automatic writing. Taking a peek into the future you. Again, AWE can show the way.

When I work with a coaching client, the biggest challenge isn't a lack of thinking big, or taking steps, or even motivation. It's a hidden wound, buried deep beyond the thinking mind. Inside each of us is a subconscious filled with spiderwebs and booby-traps, just waiting to derail our dreams and keep us small. It's not the subconscious's fault. Its job is to remember wounds and dangers and keep us out of harm's way. And, unfortunately, keep us small.

They say the thinking mind accounts for at most 10 percent of what we can get done, and the subconscious the other 90. Now again, how in the world this is tested, I have no idea. But what it means is that if you try to will yourself to do something, force yourself to do something, or think you can get motivated to overcome any obstacle, you'll soon be likely humbled. And brought to your knees.

Why? Because the subconscious has a set point, or a comfort zone it doesn't like going beyond. And when you test that zone, it brings you back in line. If you feel you're only worthy of making $50K or even $100K a year, then each time you go beyond that, you blow things up. Feel you're not worthy of love? Then each time you get into a relationship, it's with that same girl or guy who ends up treating you like crap. Or in our case, whenever the going got really good, suddenly chaos would appear—before I renegotiated things in AWE, that is. Why? Because my set point wasn't comfortable with success.

The answer here isn't necessarily more therapy or more willpower. You need to rewire your subconscious. Now it helps to also clear wounds. AWE can help you with this as well. Yes, in essence, AWE can be your own personal Freud, Maslow, or Jung (he's my favorite, because he understood the waking world is the dream world, and the dream world is the waking). For when we learn how to work with the subconscious, we become truly unstoppable.

One way we can move past our subconscious blocks is literally to go into AWE and ask what they are. For you can't easily clear something you're not even aware of. So you can ask in AWE, "What are my biggest blocks?" or "What's holding me back?" or "Why do I keep shooting myself in the foot?" or "Why does it seem like I'm doing the one-two-cha-cha-cha in life, that each time I take one step forward, I'm taking two steps back?" In AWE you'll get the answers, but that's only half the battle.

From here, you need to learn how to clear it. Now in addition to finding a talented coach or counselor who specializes in reprogramming the subconscious, you can directly ask AWE as your coach: "How do I clear this?" or "What do I do?" AWE will often quite literally give you exercises or homework to do, often far better than anything any expert could generically offer.

Talking about dreaming big, I like to mention two former top execs from Google X (Tom Chi, co-founder, and Mo Gawdat, former chief business officer) who were guests on my *Inspire Nation* show. Google X (now called X) is the division where they do outrageous things, like work on self-driving cars, which are no longer seen as so outrageous, and reach for the stars. They call these kinds of dreams moonshots. To listen to their moonshot interviews visit www.InspireNationShow.com.

Mantras, Affirmations, and the Hypnagogic State

One of the most powerful tools we have at our disposal is affirmations, though not in the way people typically use them. When we use affirmations during the waking hours, it may take decades to make a difference. Picture the main character Andy Dufresne in the movie *Shawshank Redemption*. How long did it take him to carve a tunnel through the cement wall of his prison cell with a tiny rock hammer? You get the idea. You'll likely break out of prison if the guards of your mind don't catch you and sabotage you, but it'll take a very, very long time.

However, if you use your subconscious while in AWE, you're already partially on the other side of the veil where the mind is far softer and more malleable. Couple it with the hypnagogic state, that half-awake, half-asleep state you enter twice a day, first thing in the morning and last thing at night, and now you're talking. Here you can carve into your subconscious like a knife into hot butter, and that's what we're shooting for.

First let me clarify: mantras and affirmations. An affirmation is a basic phrase or statement you can use to imprint or change your sub-conscious—it is the meaning, rather than the frequency, that helps it work. Conversely, a mantra has a specific frequency to it, that is often more important than the meaning of the words. It could come from Buddhism, Sanskrit, from time immemorial, or could be imprinted with energy and given to you by a guru, spiritual teacher, or even by AWE. Like saying the rosary, repeating the mantra or affirmation (I use my beaded bracelet) can be done throughout your day and is par-ticularly effective in the hypnagogic state such as in AWE or just before one sleeps or after one rises.

When you use the power of a mantra or affirmation just before you sleep, you can make a massive difference in your mind. I prefer just before sleeping, because, again, I want that subconscious working on the mantra for every moment I'm asleep.

What's an appropriate mantra? Well, whatever AWE wants to give you. I love having clients go into AWE and get their own personal, private mantra. Of course, you can use an affirmation as well. What's the difference?

Mantras are often phrases that have been used since time immemorial and have a special energy or frequency to them, like the six-syllable Sanskrit mantra, "Om mani padme hum." But they can also be a personal phrase or statement given to you by a teacher, a guru, or especially by AWE.

Of course, you can also use an affirmation, and some of them are quite powerful. One of my all-time favorites is also one of the most well known. In this situation, may I suggest the words of French psychologist Émile Coué who introduced this beautiful affirmation, which you may have heard: "Every day, in every way, I'm getting better and better. Every day, in every way, I'm getting better and better." You may adopt this one or ask in AWE for your own personal mantra.

Your subconscious then works on that as you're sleeping, helping either to fill in that groove in the record or to create more positive grooves in the record. You can literally even ask in your automatic writing before you go to bed for a mantra that you can repeat before going to sleep that will help you to heal emotional wounds.

You can even ask in AWE for help waking up energized and refreshed. It might give you a mantra similar to what I've gotten. "I wake happy, energized, and refreshed, happy, energized and refreshed, happy, energized and refreshed." When you use this and wake in the morning, you'll probably still hear yourself going, "Happy, energized, and refreshed. Happy, energized, and refreshed."

You could repeat an affirmation to help you overcome self-loathing or self-anger or some healing to do with your self-worth. And it could be: "Each day I like myself more. Each day I like myself more. Each day I like myself more." And you go to bed saying, "Each day I like myself more. Each day I like myself more." And you'll find yourself waking up repeating that mantra as well. And liking yourself more.

Ask AWE for a personal mantra. Ask for assistance and guidance before you go to sleep. Rewire your subconscious through AWE, particularly before you sleep. Then you can kick back, relax, and rewire your mind and subconscious, without having to do a thing. How does it get any better than that?

What's Your Mission (Statement)?

I'm always transmuting or transforming energy, from negative to positive, from challenges to opportunities, and taking the blank-slate energy of the day and transforming it to a powerful energy of creation. This means I like to stay in a state of intention, each and every day. For it is intention that transforms energy into matter.

What's this mean? It means knowing what's most important to you, and each day asking where you're going in the world. That means having a mission statement, and writing it out each day in AWE. What's a mission statement? It's who you are, what you stand for, and what you want to be remembered for, or how you want to remember your life at the very end of it.

It's not something that needs dramatic specificity, though that's certainly not bad. But the more you can hone in on who you are and what you stand for, the more direction you'll find each day and the more doors that open up, because the Universe rewards focused energy. I like to say focused concentration equals power. Or as my dear friend and author Mitch Horowitz brilliantly wrote in *The Miracle Habits*, concentration produces power.

So how do you come up with your mission statement? I'd recommend bringing it to AWE. Spend twenty to thirty minutes, or more, one morning writing out at least a page about your mission statement. Then work over a week or two to shorten it, first to two paragraphs, then to one, and by the end of two weeks, see if you can get it to a few short sentences. The more you do this in AWE, the tighter and more insightful your statement will be.

Here's my mission statement, though, I must say, Jessica's been challenging me to get even more specific with it myself:

> To raise people's vibrations, elevate humanity, and shift consciousness, through my books, speaking, teaching, and mentoring world leaders and great change makers, while traveling and exploring the world, meeting indigenous elders, and spending more time with friends and family, in the creative process, running and playing in nature—becoming even healthier and stronger, continuing my spiritual development, and growing the closest connection to Spirit I possibly can. Spirit is my oxygen.

Note, I did not include specifics about a show or coaching. Why? Because these are simply vehicles for my mission. The show is "merely" a beautiful, amazing vehicle to help me achieve my mission. While I want to be specific, I want to leave wiggle-room for the Universe to steer me where she wishes, to help me complete my mission.

Once you've got your mission statement, I want you to write it down each and every session in AWE until it's absolutely burned into your psyche and where you could answer it to anyone, at any time, at the drop of a hat.

The next step is to ask in AWE what your single-minded purpose is for the day, one that fits within your personal mission statement. You will recall I introduced the SMP into the AWE ritual early on. In this way, each day you are assured of making tiny steps and occasionally big leaps toward fulfilling your mission. Then you won't wonder on your death bed what you did with your life.

A last note, while I love Napoleon Hill's *Think and Grow Rich*, he encourages you to write the equivalent of your mission statement on an index card and reread it multiple times a day. I differ with this advice, in that I want you to write it out in AWE each and every day, if not two or three times a day.

There's an energy of writing it out, and there's an energy of rethinking it. My mission statement, and yours as well, will change and grow over time. And that's perfect. It does not need to be rigid at all. Instead you want to follow the energy. When you're simply reading it, that's rote energy. It's flat, it's autopilot, and it could almost feel meaningless. But when you have to rewrite it, and think about it, and most importantly feel about it, then there's an energy and excitement that helps draw you toward that future.

The Beauty of "or Something Better!" and How to Attract Surprises

While we're on the topic of manifesting and attracting goodness into your life, let me offer one more practice with AWE I think you will like. I want to teach you one simple tool that you can use in AWE to help you attract something even greater than you could ever possibly have imagined.

At the end of any automatic writing when I do prayer and manifestation work, I always say, *"For my highest good, the highest good of all, or something better."* Those three simple words, *or something better,* allow the Universe to bring you something greater than you have ever imagined.

For instance, we can be a tiny seed and think I want to grow up to be the biggest, boldest, most powerful seed that we can possibly imagine, having no idea that instead of just being a little seed, we can actually be a mighty sequoia—a gigantic, incredible tree that reaches almost to the heavens.

But if we say, "I want to be a big seed, I want to be a big seed, I want to be a big seed," and hold on tight to that demand of the Universe, then we never actually allow the Universe to plant us in the ground and water us. Instead, we don't let go, and we hold onto our shell. But if we say, "or something better," we are telling the Universe, I surrender, I let go, I give it to you, Universe, God, or whoever, and we allow the magic in. Then, boom. We take off to the top of the redwood forest and beyond.

For Jessica and myself, we lived in an amazing mountain home, a log cabin A-frame with a drop-dead gorgeous view over the entire valley and town below. Each morning when we awoke, we opened the curtains, and there before us was a mountain valley view straight out of Switzerland. There was a 14,000-foot Colorado peak behind us, and an 11,000-foot volcano at our doorstep. Truly something spectacular. And certainly beyond our wildest dreams.

Jessica had come out to this valley to look for a place for us to live, away from New Jersey and North Carolina (where we moved after leaving New Jersey, renewed, refreshed). We wanted to move back to Colorado, which we have always loved. She was looking in downtown

Aspen and not finding anything. She actually made two trips out without finding a thing.

She said to me, "I think we need to let go of what we are attached to. We need to let go of what we believe is the ultimate answer to where we're supposed to live." In other words, it was time to go with the "or something better."

We'd been doing the work in AWE, but we specifically asked if there was something we were missing, something we weren't seeing, and that we were open to whatever may be best. In essence, we dropped the "must be Aspen" and asked for the "or something better."

The next thing you know, Jessica found herself two towns over from Aspen—ironically the town she'd stayed in twice at Airbnbs, marveling at the wonderful town and saying, "I never expected to be here." And when she did so, two magical homes, one even more magical than the other, appeared.

When you let go and surrender to the Universe, and to the possibility of something greater than you could ever imagine, that's just what you may get. Or something better.

Surrendering—the Key to Attracting Miracles

I am often faced with multiple demands, all at the same time, as you may be. There's literally no way to do everything at once. So what's the answer? Creative scheduling might help, but we're all faced with this overload now and again.

The answer? Surrender. Look for the path of flow, for there is always a magical path somewhere, a river of energy that makes things easier to get done. The trick is that we often hold on too tightly to what we feel is the solution. And that can hurt, and hurt badly.

To me, AWE is the ultimate practice of surrender, for you go in without attachment to what you'll hear, and you simply let your guides speak to you. If you understand just how powerful this is—in other words, showing up in life without a set agenda and letting the Universe lead the way—struggles get much easier.

Surrender's what got us our magical miracle home. Surrender's what helped us start the show, and surrender is the key to keeping us out of pain. Quite literally.

What does surrender mean? Surrender doesn't mean that you're giving up. Surrender doesn't mean that you're going to become one with the couch and say, "I give up on everything." Although that's actually not a bad place to begin.

What surrender truly means is I'm going to stop trying to push the stone uphill; I'm going to listen to the signs and symbols of the Universe; and I am going to take action accordingly.

Here's how that works: You will recall I found myself near death in a freezing creek. I had not listened to the Universe some weeks before during a series of car accidents, a broken foot, and burglary of our stuff. I didn't heed the signs. The Universe speaks first in whispers, then grabs the two-by-four, as I found out. Had I only surrendered, I may not have needed that experience, nor the additional titanium femur and hip that was to follow.

Surrender is not giving up, but listening to the signs, symbols, and energetic waves of the Universe. We want to surf those waves, not be fighting to stay beneath the tsunami, just waiting to be pounded.

When signs and symbols come to you, when you keep hitting that wall, Universe is saying pivot. And if you pivot, there is something greater, something even better likely waiting for you. In AWE you can literally say, "I surrender. I surrender." Not an "I give up," but "I give in to greater guidance from AWE, greater guidance from the Universe, greater guidance than I could possibly imagine."

Openness allows the kingdom of heaven to unlock, while holding on tight only produces pain. For to be truly open and in a state of grace, and that's what surrender is, surrender is a state of grace, to be truly open is to listen, look, and pay attention with everything you've got. And especially by taking your surrender to your automatic writing.

When the going gets tough, when the doors start closing in on you, surrender into that which is and ask for wisdom and guidance. It is there. When you're in pain, when things aren't working out, there is a magnificent, beautiful gift of guidance waiting for you. If you can stop, drop into your automatic writing and write "I surrender. I surrender. I surrender." Perhaps the two most powerful words in the Universe.

I started this chapter inviting you to view the future you in automatic writing, and then I took you through helpful exercises to reprogram your subconscious, to discover your WOO HOOs. Dreams don't have to remain dreams, especially if you tap into AWE to manifest them and to attract even your wildest dreams into your life. You may discover something even better—a gift from the Universe. Be surprised, surrender to miracles. And let your dreams come true.

13 | Increase Your Wealth with Automatic Writing

Even for the best of us, many of us have wounds or blocks around money.

Let me explain what these might be. Conscious or unconscious energetic patterns keep us in a place of lack or fear. For example, if you are living with repeating patterns where you make money and lose it, or simply find yourself having more month left at the end of your money, you could have a wound or block that gets to be cleared.

Possibly you have had this wound or block from childhood, because of an early loss or even from your parents before you. In other words, you may have inherited a wound that causes you to repeat a familial pattern of losing money as well. The clearing of old patterns can be profound, whether they revolve around money or trauma.

But a caution here: Other inherited familial or ancestral wounds (one example would be children of Holocaust survivors) are a powerful topic that AWE can help with, especially if there's a history of any sort of trauma, abuse, or challenges in your family line, but these may be a bit outside the scope of this chapter—yet one powerful way AWE can help.

The automatic writing experience (AWE) can actually be a fun and enlightening exercise or regular practice for money management. For one thing, your guides will let you know what your worries, fears, concerns, and even blind spots about money are—and that's perhaps the most important accomplishment of all.

Who has issues with money? We all do. I've even met billionaires who struggled with feelings of fear, worry, and anxiety around holding onto the money they have. So while I'm not saying you fire your accountant or bookkeeper, I encourage you to bring your money concerns, and even your budget, to automatic writing.

Beyond that, you can literally budget out your year, look at upcoming years, and even what you'd do if you have an unexpected windfall, or if you manifested extra monies through AWE. When it comes to numbers, I like to have a sharp pencil and be conservative on paper. AWE can help you find potential pitfalls and problems before they happen. And although I typically don't use the word realistic, you can be realistic about money with AWE.

How do we do that? Again, after your "What do I need to know?" question, you can open up to AWE and ask anything. I'd recommend putting your budget down, or even using a mindmap to draw out your monthly or yearly budget ahead, like this: I take a circle hub approach. At the center of the circle, or the hub, put down your month or year, then around it map out all of your expenses (mortgage, rent, car payment, utilities, insurance, food, vacation, clothing, school loans, other loans, taxes, savings, IRA, 401(k), fun money, for example). Then ask in AWE, "Is there anything I'm missing?" or "Is there anything I haven't thought about?" or even "Do these numbers seem good to you?"

If you have your own business, for example, and you're bringing in $7,500 a month, you could say, "Well, what happens if I bring in $10,000 a month?" And write it out in automatic writing and see where you would allocate funds. Ask: "What would happen if I get $12,500 or $15,000 or more?"

Granted, this is not an exercise I'd do week one of AWE, for the ego loves to get involved when it comes to money and numbers. But if you've established a good relationship and can see when ego's sneaking in the game, then AWE will give you useful answers about your numbers. Key point: AWE is not a registered accountant, attorney, or certified financial planner—nor am I—so you may want to check your numbers with a pro. But with that said, AWE will let you know when you're embellishing or if you're out to lunch, being overly optimistic, or even missing an entire category of something.

For myself, there've been times my writing has wanted me to be more conservative, and then, in other times, it's like I'm taking the leap of faith, for example, to buy my Tesla a few years back, when it said, "Go! Go! Go!"

In essence, you could have a business discussion in automatic writing with your intuition or higher self as to where you would spend the revenue, how you would best allocate your funds, and different ways to prioritize what you'll do based on how much money you have. With AWE, you've got a high-level business advisor to help you plan and prioritize.

Using AWE is a fascinating way to get a big-picture perspective on money and one that steps past, or even above, the worries, fears, and concerns of your egoic or "small" mind, and instead takes a bigger picture, "big" mind or holistic perspective on how and where to place your money in life.

On that note, in addition to our online AWE course (www.Automatic Writing.com), we have several courses that came through in AWE on the alchemy of money and how to transform your relationship with money. They can be found on our website (www.InspireNation University.com).

This exercise in AWE can literally take you down to the dollars and cents of budgeting. If you're on a tight budget, if you're trying to make it through, put it out there in automatic writing and ask specifically, "What do I put where?" and "What's the best way to get through this time?" And, of course, I would always ask: "Can you show me how kind, gentle, and easy more money can come in? What is the way I can have more of the resources I need to get things done, to live the lifestyle I want to live, to make it through this time period, and to thrive in the future?"

Not a single day goes by where I'm in automatic writing that I'm not either talking about finances or wealth and abundance. Abundance is your birthright. You don't have to be ashamed or embarrassed or say to yourself, "This is something spiritual. I shouldn't be asking for money." It's a common challenge for us spiritual folk, so let me set the record straight.

Money is spiritual. Money is energetic currency. It's energy. And it's yours to help yourself and help others in need. The higher vibration you hold, the more money you have the potential to bring into your life, and money allows you to help more people.

The Universe works with the law of reciprocity. So when you do work, and you do not ask for an even exchange of money in return (we're not talking volunteer work, that brings its own energy in return), then you will not be rewarded by the Universe. You must value yourself by asking for what you're worth, or the Universe cannot give you what you value.

Calling in money with AWE is a two-step dance: First, you ask, and then you have to step forward to do something to bring in money. That's reciprocity, and it's important.

But ask, ask, ask, ask, ask.

Wealth and abundance doesn't just have to do with money. It applies to many areas of your life. Let's now examine eight specific wealth categories.

Write Down Your WOO HOO 8

If you ever see the license plate on my shiny yellow Tesla (with gold wheels for fun, of course, because the wheels make the vehicle—and make people smile)—WOO HOO 8—you will now know what it means (unlike the bazillion other people who stop and ask me all the time) because I am going to explain how to use the WOO HOO 8 manifestation technique. Why do I have WOO HOO 8 on my vehicle? Because it's using the technique I'm about to teach you (and the one I used to draw Tessie into my life).

You can use this tool with AWE to draw yourself toward almost anything you desire, whether that's a car, a relationship, a baby, a new job, or just about anything you desire. Of course, it all depends on whether it's for your highest good and the highest good of all.

The WOO HOO 8 exercise is the number-one tool I teach all of my clients when it comes to abundance, manifestation, or simply calling in much-needed goodness, in just about any area of your life. It's called the WOO HOO 8 because you work in eight different categories of life, and the WOO HOO because that's the energy you're going to bring to these areas.

I recommend doing this in AWE just after you've asked the "Who am I?" question, or just before you ask for your SMP. (You can find out more about when to start adding questions or changing things up in the 30-Day Challenge chapter up next.)

You want to write about these eight specific categories. I put these in terms of "wealth" because wealth encompasses far more than just your money in the bank.

1. **Time Wealth:** If you have all the money in the world, but you don't have time to live, breathe, or just be, then your money's not worth anything.

2. **Health Wealth:** If you don't have health, then no matter how much money you have, it's not worth a thing. To quote the Dalai Lama here: "Man. Because he sacrifices his health in order to make money. Then he sacrifices money to recuperate his health. And then he is so anxious about the future that he does not enjoy the present; the result being that he does not live in the present or the future; he lives as if he is never going to die, and then dies having never really lived."

3. **Financial Wealth:** While they say money can't buy you happiness, it is still important in this material world. And studies in the US show that at least until you make up to $75,000 annually, money actually can make you happier. Most of all, it's an amplifier. What you are before you're wealthy is what you'll get more of. So if you're happy before wealth, chances are you'll find yourself happier. And if you're miserable, you'll find yourself even more so. It's yet another reason to do the work in AWE.

4. **Family and Friends Wealth:** If ever the importance of having a network or a safety net is apparent, it's during tough times such as the pandemic. We realized how important it was to have real friends, and family that has your back, and know you have theirs. On our death bed, chances are we won't be talking about the cars we have or anything else of the sort, but of our relationships, and our time with loved ones, including beloved pets.

5. **Spiritual or Inner Wealth:** To me, this is perhaps the most important. For I want to remember that I'm a spiritual being, having a human experience each and every moment. It's so easy to forget, but when I can remember to remain plugged in, it changes the tenor of everything. And inner wealth reduces stress and anxiety, eliminates depression, and returns us to our natural, happy state of beingness. Imagine feeling connected and positive nearly all of the time.

6. **Business or Career Wealth:** Human nature is to be productive, to do something worthwhile, meaningful, and feel like we're making a difference. When we work on our business or career wealth, we are engaging in the creative process for our lives and the lives of those around us. At the end of the day, whether we're working in the office, building our own empire, or raising our kids (certainly a massive career undertaking all to itself), we are finding ways to serve and help others. And we're fulfilling a need for growth, for challenge, and to see what impact we can make on the world. When we grow our business and career wealth, we feel much better.

7. **Creative Wealth:** When you're inspired or in-spirit, you completely lose track of time, minutes, hours, and even days. It doesn't matter whether that's singing, dancing, painting, sculpting, telling jokes, writing books, building a business, making a rolling rooster coop (okay, just made that one up, but why not?), nearly anything can be creative if you want it to be so. This is your God time, this is when you're so fully connected, you lose track of almost everything and everyone

around you. You're plugged into the fire hose of the Universe, and you see things, feel things, and even often understand things in a completely different way. The more we're plugged in creatively, the better we feel about everything. We simply need to give ourselves permission to do so, and make it a regular part of our lives. Yes, when you're plugged into that creative side, the answers begin to flow.

8. **Home, Nature, and Travel Wealth:** Having a special roost, or sacred place to call home, is so important, and at a time when the entire world is spinning, perhaps more important now than ever. And being connected to the earth is especially important during this time too. Whether you're out exploring and finding new lands, being grounded in the home, or rooted in nature, having home, nature, and travel wealth gives you a foundation for greater well-being and can be the hub you need to build the greatest wheel in your life. For when you feel grounded, have found your earth, and can stretch your natural exploration instinct that's buried inside of each and every one of us, it positively peppers our entire existence. And from there, we feel capable of doing almost anything.

So now that you know the eight categories, let's talk about how you work with them.

The WOO HOO 8 is a powerful life-long process—meaning, once you start, you won't want to stop. When we lived in North Carolina and began dreaming of the mountains, I began using the WOO HOO 8 for one to two hours a day. I just wanted to see and envision the future that was already waiting for me and help call it in. It was a fun process, and I enjoyed kicking back, dreaming, and getting it all down.

That's key with the WOO HOO 8. It gets to be a fun process, first and foremost. If you're writing about your future and it doesn't feel good, then stop. And either come back to it another time or ask why this doesn't feel good. For e-motion, or energy in motion, is essential to create anything in life. And there's nothing more powerful than positive e-motion.

Let's begin by working with one WOO HOO 8 category a day. I suggest you take them in order, from category 1 to 8.

Whenever you do your automatic writing, before you ask "What's my SMP?" dive into a category. Then write about it with everything you've got from a place of emotion. Get yourself really excited. For instance, if it's home wealth, imagine your new home, up in the mountains or in a cozy condo or three-bedroom suburban neighborhood or spacious apartment in the city. WOO HOO!

Dream big, imagine big, get incredibly excited—whatever that means for you. But get those emotional juices flowing. And paint a picture of the most incredible future, or home, or spiritual wealth, or time wealth. Put the most magnificent picture on paper and in your mind's eye that you possibly can. And the more emotion you can bring to it the better.

So for each of the next eight days, take one category a day and write at least a page on it. (Or you can follow along with the 30-Day Challenge in the next chapter.) A page about your new home, what it looks like, how it makes you feel, and why it'd be so phenomenal. No, you don't have to have the specifics, just get the emotions down and let yourself dream.

For instance, I know we're building a business to change the world, but I don't pretend to know exactly how it's coming about. But I can get in that feeling state, a sense of confidence, of accomplishment, and a knowingness that I'm making a difference. I know there will be more books, and speaking, and traveling, and even meetings with world leaders—which started with an invitation to attend the World Summit of Nobel Peace Laureates in 2019.

So I get this down, and I imagine it, and feel it, even without knowing the exact details, but it helps bring it about, which, to me, of course, means calling myself to a future that already exists. For when you get clarity of emotion in your mind's eye, it unlocks the door to a future that's already there.

Here's an example of a few sentences from each of the eight categories:

Time Wealth

Thank you for my time to write, my time to be, my time to spend with my family. Thank you for all the free time in the world. I find myself growing wealthier and wealthier, while having much more time. There's time to explore, to play, to feel free. To meet with Mayan elders, to explore my cenote visions, to travel the world without time commitments holding me back. And thank you for the time to sit, to be with Jessica, to be with the animals, and be with nature, without feeling I'm supposed to be somewhere, or do something, but to simply be present for as long as I desire.

Health Wealth

I find myself growing stronger and stronger, able to run mountains, my knees feel so incredibly healthy on the downhills. My teeth are strong, my digestion is getting better and better. I have so much incredible energy for my work, for the kitties, for our rooster, and for all of the beautiful work I want to do in the world. I can run marathons with ease. I am growing stronger and stronger still. I feel so powerful, so capable, so young! How does it get any better than this? WOO HOO!

Financial Wealth

Thank you for my incredible abundance. Thank you for us having the money to have the most magnificent mountain home, ocean home, and the ability to travel anywhere we want at any time. Thank you for the ability to help people, to serve with our money to be philanthropists, and to build and give to organizations that are making a tremendous difference in the world. I feel wealthy, I feel abundant, and I feel free! WOO HOO!

Family and Friends Wealth

Thank you for my tribe, for my family, for us finding a village to call home. Thank you for the time to spend with family, to cultivate greater friendships, and to grow even closer to those we love. Thank you for our healthy happy babies! Thank you for the tribe to raise our children! Thank you for the love and support from others, and for the love and support we have to share. We feel loved, we feel supported, we feel community, and we feel ohana. Thank you, God! WOO HOO!

Spiritual or Inner Wealth

Thank you for my spiritual connection, where I feel the love that's all around me all day long. Thank you for my remembrance that I'm a spiritual being. Thank you for my growing closer to the spirit world, and the spirit realm, and can see, hear, and feel Spirit around me even more each minute. Thank you for my staying in a place of peace, love, harmony and understanding, always in a state of equanimity, always plugged in, and always coming from the heart.

Business and Career Wealth

Thank you for our incredible business success, for our millions and millions of viewers worldwide. Thank you for our best-selling books, and book after book reaching millions each and every year. Thank you for our expanding outreach to help others even more around the globe, of having an influence to help change the planet. Of things going incredibly easily with more wealth coming in with less effort, more things on autopilot, and the most incredible dream team to help get things done.

Creative Wealth

I see myself learning to draw, and singing, and taking singing lessons and exploring all that's possible with the show, really turning it into an experience, and being on Netflix or Amazon Prime. How does it get any better than this! And making music, and writing book after book after book. Thank you for our show becoming an "experience" an out-of-the-box journey people take with us once a week. Thank you for all of my creative endeavors, thank you for my reaching others.

Home, Nature, and Travel Wealth

Thank you for our forever home animal sanctuary with places people can come to meditate, and be on retreat, and with trails, and animals, and such incredible peace, but so close to town as well, and so incredibly convenient, and is such a perfect place to raise our children. Thank you for the nature all around us, thank you for the animals, the wildlife, the trees, the trails, and the connection to the land, to the spirit of the land, and to living in a place where each morning and evening our jaws hit the floor, and we go, I can't believe we live here! And thank you for my ability to meet with world leaders, and travel around the world, helping guide others and the planet. How does it get any better than this? WOO HOO!

The Power of Gratitude

I often go back and forth on how I write my WOO HOO 8, fluidly without thought. At one point I may say "I feel" and another "thank you for." There is no one right way, and I don't believe asking for, or saying I feel, or anything other than thanks means that it isn't already here. Nothing could be further from the truth, so write it any way you'd like.

With that said, there is a power in gratitude, that truly helps bring things about. So the more you can say thanks for the things that you desire, the more you're drawing yourself toward them. You must use gratitude from a place of high vibes and emotion for it to have the full effect. Saying thank you like a Debbie Downer has no emotion and tends to fall flat.

But what if you can't bring any emotion to the practice? First, ask in AWE why: "Why do I feel flat? Why does this thing that I feel should excite me leave me feeling numb? Do I have an emotional wound or block, or is it something someone else wants, but not me?"

For instance, I once worked with the most amazing exotic dancer whose family wanted her to work in finance. Actually, she did work in finance for years, but found she felt better, had more freedom, and made more money dancing in her evenings. We're not here to judge, but to follow the pull of our heart. In AWE she wasn't getting that finance was the answer. But from what I recall, over time, there was a pull to play with the money she made.

The answer: be open, be honest with yourself, don't follow anyone else's path, but ask yourself how this feels for you. And if you can't find the emotion, bring it to AWE and find out why.

Perhaps something is not meant for you. Perhaps there's too much fear. Or a wounding from the past. Or maybe there's something inside of you from the past that's walled you off to all of it. Ask in AWE, find out, and then go to remove that wound or block with everything you've got.

After you have addressed all eight areas of wealth, I encourage you to go from writing at least a page a day, to a few sentences, combining all eight categories into one page or so. You can make this fluid, so it's not exactly two or three sentence per category, but instead following the energy.

In essence, you'll go from writing approximately a page a day per category, to a page, or even half a page total as you put it all together, flowing from one category to the next, as you help draw yourself toward your greatest future. Just remember to write with as much emotion as you can.

For your WOO HOO 8, you want big goals as well, but you want to think they're attainable, even if just barely on the grasp of attainable. Don't let your subconscious reject these ideas by making them unbelievable. You're doing this as a conscious exercise so they can be huge goals, but make sure on some level you believe they're possible.

Envision Your Future

In addition to your WOO HOO 8, you can use AWE to help sculpt, envision, and cultivate the brightest future you can imagine—or even brighter than that!

You don't need to do this every day, but this is an ideal exercise to do on your birthday, at the beginning of the year, or on the new moon, or at solstice and equinox—powerful times to plant seeds and intention for the seasons and years ahead.

On my fiftieth birthday, you can't imagine what I did to envision my future. I did an extended WOO HOO 8 to envision or draw into clarity the next fifty years of my life—or what I consider my second life for that matter—as I see fifty as a starting point for newness and greatness—in other words, a new start on life.

Just like with the WOO HOO 8, I brought emotion, but I also brought specificity, as I know where I'm going and what I'm doing, at least in the short term. I don't know the specifics of where I exactly want the business to be in ten or twenty years, but I do have a clear idea where I want to be at the end of this year, or even a year from now. And so I wrote it down, all the specifics, all the details, all the hopes, dreams, and desires. And then I wrote down longer term, and longer term still.

This is a powerful intention-setting exercise. When done in AWE, you're casting the largest stone of intention into the pond of intention. Put another way, you're creating huge ripples to wash up on your future shore, and just the way you'd like—or *something better.*

What better way to end this chapter than to let Elaine, one of my AWE students, tell her story of attracting wealth (and not just in dollars):

> Shortly after learning the process of automatic writing, I began testing out what would happen if I used the process to ask for wisdom or advice from people I admired in life, but who had passed away. Maya Angelou is a woman I admired deeply when she was living. I felt a meaningful connection to her because I am a writer, but I also benefited from the sage advice . . . When I wrote to ask her for wisdom, this is the answer I was given first:
>
> *The spider web is a perfect creation of angles and circles, a natural order of chaos and beauty. You can learn a lot from a spi-*

der. To watch one build a web is a fascinating miracle. That belly full of gleaming thread, tied along whiskers of grass or between fence posts, to be rippled by wind and sometimes torn apart, the spider simply goes back to threading another web. That single-minded dedication keeps the spider alive. She spins her web to capture insects, and without it she would not eat. Spiders are creatures of pure intent, their industry both art and survival are linked as one. There is no separation of art and life purpose. The industry of art is the purpose of life. Give yourself to art, and it will fill you with purpose and your industry will feed you.

This, of course, gave me a great deal to consider. The next day was dedicated to art I created for people I work with on a local organic farm. While that art was fun to create and give away, I have been living on shaky financial ground for over a year. My financial circumstances were troubling me, and the writing I have contributed with such passion for my craft was not making me enough money on which to live.

Maya Angelou's idea about the spider bubbled in the back of my head, feeding my heart with a sense of collecting my scattered thinking, my egoic desire to DO, DO, DO. Such a change takes time, so less than a month later I was once again asking Dr. Angelou to offer me advice in my morning automatic writing. Here is her response:

Remember the spider? Single-minded dedication to the craft of catching food. It lives in abundance while it waits for the food to come. The spider trusts that after it completes the work it is made to do, the abundance of supply will simply arrive in the web. You are doing the work, but forgetting to wait for the abundance. Make space for the abundance to come. Open yourself wide to the nourishment of the Universe. You are contributing to the well-being of others, and the Universe will reward you. Think of all your work as the web, and then you will understand how it will capture the abundance of the Universe through the industry you offer.

Almost exactly one month later, the idea my son and I had been discussing about creating a regenerative farm where a tiny house community could live sustainably suddenly gained ground. Like a lightning rod, an idea to share a video about my plans came to me and I posted it on Instagram. A woman I never met in person donated $250 to me so I could start my farm! That morning I had written a request that the Universe show me a sign I was on the right trajectory, and that it would come with feathers. Right before I received the donation, I saw a post by the woman who gave me the money: she had photographed birds on the beach.

Can I say I have achieved my goals yet? Not quite, but the confirmations are like a buoy, and my heart is lifted. I feel lighter and more focused. My direction is no longer scattered, but is linear and clear. I am building a web of community, resources, and connections to begin building a means to feed people food that sequesters carbon in the soil, prevents top soil from being washed into the waterways, and has a plan for growth beyond just one community. This work has the potential to heal the ecosystems all over the planet, and in just the last few days I have had several exciting conversations about possible ways to make this vision a reality.

What only I know is that I already feel like this vision exists as reality, and now it will be built with many hands to make light work. Many hands will be industrious builders of art we create in a partnership with the earth.

14 | Take the AWE 30-Day Challenge

ow that you know the basics about automatic writing, it's time to help you dive deep, create a life-long habit, and give you the best way to ensure your automatic writing success.

This thirty-day program is designed to help you quickly get into AWE and into the basics, without being overwhelmed. Stick to this challenge as best you can and you will become an automatic writing superstar.

I encourage you to track your progress for important insights and motivation. You may print the 30-Day Challenge worksheet from the automatic writing website (www.AutomaticWriting.com/bonuses).

Before you begin—

1. Prepare to get up and write in the morning or before bed in the evening and choose a regular time and sacred space for your automatic writing for the next thirty days.

2. Choose your writing instrument and a journal to begin, or the computer/device you will use to type.

3. Download theta brain-entrainment music for your practice from the automatic writing website (www.AutomaticWriting.com/bonuses).

Here are the explanations for each column on the chart:

DAY: Use the entry for each consecutive day, from day 1 to day 30.

ASSIGNMENT: In the beginning, start off with the basics and repetition so you can get in the groove and feel more confident. By the end of thirty days, the order of your automatic writing will look something like this:

1. Intention Prayer
2. Invocation Prayer
3. "What do I need to know today?"
4. "Who am I?" (for the first two weeks only, then optional)
5. Optional Questions (begins on day 7)
6. "What's my SMP?"
7. WOO HOO 8 (begins on day 20)

The entire process will typically take twenty to thirty minutes (plus a few minutes of reading midday or in the evening), but will be well worth it for how it sets you up for success for your day, week, year, and life, and how much better you feel through the process—not to mention all of the wins you'll attract into your life.

ACTIVITY: Record what time you start writing. This may give you a better clue as to the best automatic writing time for you. Don't worry about writing in both the morning and evening. One or the other is fine for now. I've included the PM slot for people who work nightshifts or if doing AWE in the AM doesn't work for you.

DONE: When you complete an activity, check it as complete. Checking things off just makes you feel good.

MINUTES: In the last column, record the number of minutes you spent writing. This may also motivate you and give you guidance as to the best time to write.

The AWE 30-Day Challenge

DAY	ASSIGNMENT	ACTIVITY	DONE	MINUTES
1	Begin automatic writing with 3 basic questions, allowing for at least 5 minutes per question: What do I need to know today? Who am I? What's my SMP, or my Single-Minded Purpose, for the day?	AM Write __:___ am Midday Read PM Write __:___ pm	√	
2	Continue with the 3 basic questions, allowing for at least 5 minutes per question: What do I need to know today? Who am I? What's my SMP, or my Single-Minded Purpose, for the day?	AM Write __:___ am Midday Read PM Write __:___ pm		
3	Continue with the 3 basic questions, allowing for 5–10 minutes per question: What do I need to know today? Who am I? What's my SMP, or my Single-Minded Purpose, for the day?	AM Write __:___ am Midday Read PM Write __:___ pm		
4	Continue with the 3 basic questions, allowing for 5–10 minutes per question (or more if you feel like the words are flowing): What do I need to know today? Who am I? What's my SMP, or my Single-Minded Purpose, for the day?	AM Write __:___ am Midday Read PM Write __:___ pm		

DAY	ASSIGNMENT	ACTIVITY	DONE	MINUTES
5	Continue with the 3 basic questions: What do I need to know today? Who am I? What's my SMP, or my Single-Minded Purpose for the day?	AM Write __:__ am		
		Midday Read		
		PM Write __:__ pm		
6	Repeat: What do I need to know today? Who am I? What's my SMP, or my Single-Minded Purpose for the day?	AM Write __:__ am		
		Midday Read		
		PM Write __:__ pm		
Note	Beginning with Day 7, you may begin adding optional questions about yourself. It's recommended to ask at least one new question daily. With each day are suggested questions. However, feel free to ask different questions, OR change the order, OR continue with one question for multiple days.			
7	Ask the following Optional Question after asking "Who am I?" and before asking "What's my SMP?" Is there anything I need to know to take better care of myself?	AM Write __:__ am		
		Midday Read		
		PM Write __:__ pm		
8	Ask the following Optional Question after asking "Who am I?" and before asking "What's my SMP?" Is there anything I need to know to take better care of my health?	AM Write __:__ am		
		Midday Read		
		PM Write __:__ pm		

DAY	ASSIGNMENT	ACTIVITY	DONE	MINUTES
9	Ask the following Optional Question after asking "Who am I?" and before asking "What's my SMP?" Is there anything else I need to know to take better care of my friends and family?	AM Write __:__ am		
		Midday Read		
		PM Write __:__ pm		
10	Ask the following Optional Question after asking "Who am I?" and before asking "What's my SMP?" What is my big picture purpose in life?	AM Write __:__ am		
		Midday Read		
		PM Write __:__ pm		
11	Ask the following Optional Question after asking "Who am I?" and before asking "What's my SMP?" What am I here to do at this point in my life?	AM Write __:__ am		
		Midday Read		
		PM Write __:__ pm		
12	Ask the following Optional Question after asking "Who am I?" and before asking "What's my SMP?" Is there anything I'm not realizing about my current situation in life?	AM Write __:__ am		
		Midday Read		
		PM Write __:__ pm		

DAY	ASSIGNMENT	ACTIVITY	DONE	MINUTES
13	Ask the following Optional Questions after asking "Who am I?" and before asking "What's my SMP?"	AM Write ___:___ am		
	If I'm feeling stuck, why is this, what do I need to learn and what do I need to do differently?	Midday Read		
	If I'm repeating a current pattern, ask why is this, and what do I need to do to change this?	PM Write ___:___ pm		
14	Ask the following Optional Questions after asking "Who am I?" and before asking "What's my SMP?"	AM Write ___:___ am		
	Ask, even if it does not appear to apply:	Midday Read		
	Are there any immediate blocks to my moving ahead?	PM Write ___:___ pm		
	If so, how do I begin to clear these blocks?			
15	Ask the following Optional Questions **instead** of asking "Who am I?" and before asking "What's my SMP?"	AM Write ___:___ am		
	(You don't need to ask "Who am I? anymore unless you desire.):	Midday Read		
	Are there any deep-seated wounds that need to be addressed?	PM Write ___:___ pm		
	What do I do to address these wounds?			
16	Ask the following Optional Question before asking "What's my SMP?"	AM Write ___:___ am		
	Is there anything else I need to know about my career/job or trajectory in life?	Midday Read		
		PM Write ___:___ pm		

DAY	ASSIGNMENT	ACTIVITY	DONE	MINUTES
17	Ask the following Optional Question before asking "What's my SMP?" How do I bring more abundance/prosperity into my life?	AM Write __:__ am		
		Midday Read		
		PM Write __:__ pm		
18	Ask the following Optional Questions before asking "What's my SMP?" Are there any blocks to abundance I need to remove? If so, what do I do to remove these blocks?	AM Write __:__ am		
		Midday Read		
		PM Write __:__ pm		
19	In addition to asking "What's my SMP for the day?" ask: What's my SMP for the next 3 months? What's my SMP for the year?	AM Write __:__ am		
		Midday Read		
		PM Write __:__ pm		
Note	You can continue asking a new question a day, and feel free to choose your own questions. However, now before asking "What's my SMP?" you want to begin writing your WOO HOO 8. Here are suggested categories, add one new category a day until you're writing all each daily.			
20	WOO HOO #1—HEALTH WEALTH Spend 5–10 minutes writing in detail about your health goals, what they look like, and how they will make you feel—visualize and get really excited about this, until you're almost WOO HOO'ing in your chair.	AM Write __:__ am		
		Midday Read		
		PM Write __:__ pm		

DAY	ASSIGNMENT	ACTIVITY	DONE	MINUTES
21	WOO HOO #2—TIME WEALTH Spend 5–10 minutes writing in detail about how much free time you'd like to have, what you would do with this time, and how it would make you feel. Again, get so excited about this you're going WOO HOO in your chair!	AM Write __:___ am		
		Midday Read		
		PM Write __:___ pm		
22	WOO HOO #3—ABUNDANCE or FINANCIAL WEALTH Spend 5–10 minutes writing in detail about your financial goals, what they look like, and how they will make you feel, and what you'd like to do with the additional resources you bring in. Visualize and get really excited about this until you're almost WOO HOO'ing in your chair.	AM Write __:___ am		
		Midday Read		
		PM Write —:___ pm		
23	WOO HOO #4—FAMILY & FRIENDS WEALTH Spend 5–10 minutes writing in detail about how you'd like to improve or change your relationships with various friends and family, what it would look like, why it's important, and how incredible it would make you feel.	AM Write __:___ am		
		Midday Read		
		PM Write —:___ pm		
24	WOO HOO #5—SPIRITUAL OR INNER WEALTH Spend 5–10 minutes writing in detail about how you'd like to deepen your practice or inner wisdom, what that would look like and how it would make you feel.	AM Write __:___ am		
		Midday Read		
		PM Write __:___ pm		

DAY	ASSIGNMENT	ACTIVITY	DONE	MINUTES
25	WOO HOO #6—BUSINESS OR CAREER WEALTH Spend 5–10 minute)s writing in detail about what you'd like your business or career to look like in the future, and even a next step or two, or goal or two on the path. And of course write about how incredible it would make you feel.	AM Write __:__ am Midday Read PM Write __:__ pm		
26	WOO HOO #7—CREATIVE WEALTH Spend 5–10 minutes writing in detail about what creative outlet you'd like in your life, and what you'd like that to look like and of course how incredible that would make you feel.	AM Write __:__ am Midday Read PM Write __:__ pm		
27	WOO HOO #8—HOME, NATURE & TRAVEL WEALTH Spend 5–10 minutes writing in detail about where, what, or how you'd like your home to be, change, look like, or if you're moving, where and what that would look like. Remember, you are your land, so write down where you're most connected to the earth, where you'd like to explore, or how much you'd like to get to the outdoors. And if you'd like to travel, write down where, and what draws you there or excites you about it.	AM Write __:__ am Midday Read PM Write __:__ pm		

DAY	ASSIGNMENT	ACTIVITY	DONE	MINUTES
28	Beginning today, combine all 8 categories by writing only a sentence or two per category and letting it flow together. Do this each and every morning.	AM Write __:___ am		
		Midday Read		
		PM Write __:___ pm		
29	In addition to your WOO HOO 8, ask: Is there anything missing or that I've forgotten in my life?	AM Write __:___ am		
		Midday Read		
		PM Write __:___ pm		
30	Last but not least, is to ask one of the most challenging questions **you'll ever face**, but so powerful in setting you free: Is there anything I need to forgive myself for, or anyone else in my life I need to forgive?	AM Write __:___ am		
		Midday Read		
		PM Write __:___ pm		

The AWE process is a journey in self-discovery. The more you learn about your true authentic self, aka, your higher self, the more you come to know God, Source, Universe, Divine Love, or your own interpretation of a higher power.

How does it get any better than this?

If you feel inspired, we'd love to hear about your personal experience. Please feel free to reach out at our website and share your story (www.AutomaticWriting.com).

15 | Use Automatic Writing to Go Beyond This World

I communicate with the dead.

When I first wrote this book, I wasn't sure whether to put this chapter in here or not. Would it be too out there, too woo-woo, or simply the final straw for people who think I'm completely nuts? But during this period of great evolution for humanity, where I feel we have to be our authentic selves for ourselves and the world, I had to write this. For as I mentioned in the introduction, I'm an angels guy, and I really do communicate with the dead.

Not just any dead, mind you, but loved ones in my family who have passed on, three special mentors, and one incredibly dear pet.

My pet's name is Molé and he crossed over just about a year ago as I write this. As crazy as it sounds, he was a pet vole whom we rescued one day on the trail. At the time he was four days old, couldn't open his eyes, and was stumbling around lost with heat exhaustion. I had to walk with him in my hands six miles down a steep mountain trail with fallen trees and multiple debris fields from winter avalanches, before getting him back to the car. Miraculously, we had a syringe in the car from trying to feed or save another animal, and Jessica was able to get water into him. We nursed him back to health and watched him grow up to be a mighty vole. But soon after, he passed away, and far too young.

However, after his passing, I reached out to him in AWE. And he came through loud and clear. His first words were something to the effect that he's in heaven and that he's running and playing and jumping like he never could before. And he said something quite profound, which let me know it wasn't my imagination, he said that to jump in heaven, you don't push off, you simply let go of the ground and take flight. To me, that was beyond anything I'd ever thought of.

So now I write to Molé almost daily. He's always a beacon of bright and shiny light, always with a pick-me-up, and no matter how my day is going, or how daunting the day ahead, he always has special words to cheer me up and let me know everything will be all right.

In addition to writing to Molé, I write to three very special loved ones who've all crossed over to the other side. First, there's Jack, the best man at our wedding at age eighty-nine. He was my biggest supporter and critic when he felt I was off path, for he felt I was supposed to write and speak and teach like Wayne Dyer. And he wouldn't accept anything less.

When Jessica and I wrote the books *Barefoot Running*, and later *Barefoot Walking*, he thought we were nuts, and even tried to get us to sell everything and move to St. Benedict's Monastery in Snowmass, Colorado. We did go and check it out during our last chance to visit him in Boulder, and while we didn't join the monastery (I believe it was men only, but boy did they have great chocolate chip cookies), we did end up moving nearby.

I now write to Jack daily, and he gives guidance on my work, on where I'm going, and, most importantly, on "take better care of that baby doll." For he'll give me a cosmic smack-down, aka lecture from the other side, if I'm not treating Jessica exceptionally well.

Then there's Auntie Pua, a Hawaiian *kupuna* or spiritual elder and leader, who passed away far too soon. She's always there for me on the other side, with a voice of love, and tenderness, and always wanting to share and have me teach the spirit of aloha. She's such a kind, loving voice, especially when I need it most.

And then there's our dear, dear friend, and former client Carla, who passed away just weeks after attending a Dr. Joe Dispenza event with Jessica. I can still hear her laughter and cosmic sense of humor even with her on the other side. Actually, I believe she "gets" the cosmic joke now and always wants me to take things less seriously.

There are others as well, and those who want to come through. There are spirits of past presidents, and spirit elders, and even a grandma, whom I struggled with growing up. Her name is Mildred Kramer, and she wants to talk with me. I'm still healing my heart from this one, but I know, when the time is right, she has so much to share. I really get to listen.

Connect with Your Loved Ones and the Deceased on the Other Side

To connect with loved ones on the other side is so much easier than you could ever believe. The biggest challenge is actually that—belief. For they'll typically come through, loud and clear. Whether it's a pet, a mentor, or a dear family member, they do have words to share. We just have to be willing to listen, to ask, and to suspend disbelief.

How do you do so? I include them in my invocation prayer. Invocation means to call in. So when you write to the angels, to your guides, and to your team, write to your loved ones on the other side. For instance, I'll write, "Good morning, Archangel Michael, Archangel Rafael, Archangel Gabriel. Good morning, Molé (*Hi, Daddy!*), good morning, Jack! (*Good morning, Michael!*), good morning, Auntie Pua (*aloha, dear one*), and good morning, Carla (I can hear her laugh)," and then you can single one out and simply write to him or her, ask how they're doing, what they're up to, or what they'd like to share.

For many this has become quite the profound practice, to where they've grown even closer with loved ones on the other side than they were when they were here.

How do you tell if you're making it up or not? Feel into it. How does it make you feel? Does it feel true to you? Of course, you can literally ask in AWE if you're making things up, or who is really speaking to you. And know that, not once, will you hear a judging, chastising, or shaming voice from the other side. That's just not happening. They may have stern words for you—boy has Jack on occasion! But it will always be out of love. And yes, Jack, I'll work on taking even better care of Jessica. But I'm writing, and you'd be proud—*yes, I am.*

One of the participants in my automatic writing classes, Janet, told me, "The automatic writing helps me feel connected to gratitude, my ancestors, the planet, God, and the Universe, and to myself." She shared this image of one of the pages in her journal (opposite page).

She explained, "The first paragraph of appreciation to God/ Universe opens up my heart and sometimes I just keep writing about everything I am feeling grateful for on that day. It is as if I open a faucet to how lucky I feel I really am, even in challenging times.

"The second paragraph of welcoming the earth, the archangels, St. Francis, my angels and guides and then all of the ancestors helps me feel connected to such a powerful force. It reminds me of when I was a little girl and my father would lead me in a prayer that started, 'And God bless Jeff and Ricky and Mommy and Daddy,' and we would go on to bless all of my relatives and friends. These people have now passed on, so as I remember and name them each morning, I truly feel their presence, their guidance, and their protection. What a lovely way to start the day."

Janet's journal page.

How Automatic Writing Works without Writing–aka Channeling

How does AWE work without writing? I'll explain.

I'm known for intuitive interviews. Guest after guest compliment me after the show saying it was the best interview they've ever had, even if they've been on *Oprah*.

How is that possible? Because I'm not operating from my small self, or thinking mind, during the interviews. Instead I'm diving into AWE, just without putting pen to paper. And I'm connected to their hearts, something that comes from practicing AWE. So I hear their thoughts, what they want to say and to share, how they're doing, and the one most important thing I have to ask.

And when I do so, when I open up my heart and listen to the interviewees, and listen to AWE with everything I've got, something magical happens. In effect, I'm listening on two channels: One, the guest's channel, for I want to truly hear them, and from the heart, and what they have to share. And two, I'm listening to the voice of AWE as well. For I've written in AWE so much, the words now flow, even without a pen.

The same can be said for my coaching sessions. It's why I have such remarkable success. Truth is, it's not me. I'm plugging in to my coaching client, and plugging into AWE. For the Universe gives me the answers and guides me where to go.

In the early days, you could literally see me pause for a moment in interviews, waiting for the words to percolate up. Or in coaching, my head would drop down as I waited, waited, and then, voila, the words were there. That was in the early days, when I had a dial-up connection to AWE, so to speak. Since then I've upgraded, it's come from all the practice, but I now have a high-speed broadband, or fiber-optic cable, and the words are nearly instantaneous, if I'm open to listen and I stop my thinking mind. For listening to another person means I have no business listening to myself. That would mean I'm not present.

Of course, when I'm doing an interview or coaching, it means I need to get grounded, and get centered, and stop listening to my thinking mind. That's a key to my success, not thinking. For at times like these, the thinking mind only gets me in trouble (and in interviews or coaching can literally be a distraction). That's a key with AWE too.

The more you practice AWE, the more the words become clear, and the easier it is to tell they're not coming from you. You start to hear that wisdom, throughout the day, not just during AWE. It requires a bit of slowing down and paying attention to what you're hearing in your head, or through your mind's eye, or even your gut, because the words of AWE typically don't come from a booming voice. But over time you'll recognize them, they become easier to decipher, and you'll find you're operating in AWE throughout the entire day.

I've literally had coaching clients and students go through my AWE courses and become professional mediums and channels. Why? Because they dove into AWE with everything they've got, and the connection grew stronger and stronger.

It's like growing a plant strong, or Jack's beanstalk. If you water it, tend to it with love, and keep focused on helping it grow, your connection to the heavens becomes remarkable.

Could you become a medium or channel. Absolutely if that's what you desire. But at the very least, the more time you spend in AWE, the clearer the voice becomes inside of you. Then you too can hear it in your conversations, on your walks, and in those difficult moments, when you need it most.

16 | Your Life-Transforming Journey

T hank you, bright and shiny beacons of light, for joining me on this journey into automatic writing. In these pages I have taken you step by step through the automatic writing experience we call AWE. We have explored the insight you can gain in your life using AWE, and I've taken you through the many exercises you can do while in automatic writing.

Yet, now, I have saved almost the best for last.

You can ask for words of wisdom for the day. And in that phrasing, I get my daily WOW when I typically ask for Words of Wisdom—nuggets of guidance I can take with me throughout my day.

Often the words of wisdom will have nothing at all to do with anything that you're consciously thinking about. Those are the coolest messages. So ask for the nuggets. Realize this, too, in the beginning automatic writing is rough. It's stutter-steppy because you're just learning to fly that plane.

Over time the voice gets louder and louder—the voice that comes out through the pen, although you may hear it as well. What's really cool is the more that you practice AWE, the deeper your relationship. For instance, I write thirty minutes to an hour a day now in automatic writing because the words I'm getting are so profound. But the practice also carries over into every area of my life.

You may find yourself in a business meeting with clearer thoughts. You might be in your head seeking the answer to "Do I do A or do I do B?" and you'll get the answers. I use automatic writing during my on-air interviews to know what questions to ask when. I use it during my coaching, not so much writing things down but being able to get the intuitive hits because I've spent so much time in the automatic writing experience.

Other people use AWE for channeling and being able to, literally, hear voices or get Divine guidance that they can share with others.

When you practice automatic writing regularly, you may experience profound changes in your life. So, too, your ability to tap into your intuition on a moment's notice goes up tremendously—more than you could ever imagine.

I encourage you to do automatic writing each and every day without fail. Make and keep AWE as part of your daily routine. No matter what comes your way, consider this the very oxygen that you breathe because, literally, nothing is more important.

Meditating on a mountainside is inspiring. But meditation does not teach you how to chop wood and carry water (in other words, live your life fully with attention to the mundane daily routine as well). Automatic writing will tell you how to chop wood, how to carry water, which to do in which order, what you're meant to be here for, where you're going, how to heal your wounds, how to take better care of your family, how to get a partner or spouse, and, for that matter, keep your partner happy, and how to find the perfect job—all of this can come out of your daily automatic writing experience.

You have just given yourself the greatest gift in the world: intuition, guidance, and direction on the highest level. WOO HOO!

From Me to We—Where Do We Go from Here?

As Dr. Ervin Laszlo, a dear friend and two-time Nobel Peace Prize nominee, likes to say, humanity is at a great bifurcation, meaning a powerful split in the road. And humanity can go one of two ways. She can drive herself right off the cliff, or she can elevate to a new level of consciousness. Such a profound observation especially now as the world emerges from a pandemic.

I believe the swirling energies of this time have the potential to help us evolve. To quote Paul Selig's guides who talk extensively about this time and the choices facing humanity, this is a time where we get to choose the upper room, or that place of higher vibration.

Automatic writing or AWE is a key critical component in our evolution. Why? Because to make this shift, we get to believe in something greater than ourselves, and we get to tap in. Quite literally, the more you go into AWE, the more you help all of humanity. Why? Because everything is about energy, and as you dive into AWE, your frequency goes up, and when it goes up, it helps raise the vibration or the frequency of everyone around you. It's as if you're in the orchestra and playing at a higher octave.

When you're in AWE, you feel better, drop your guard, open your heart, and act with greater kindness and compassion. Yes, you truly become an open-hearted warrior, viewing the world from a deeper, richer, more connected lens.

And it is from this place that we bring each other up.

It's a time of going from competition to cooperation. For Mother Earth has hit the red button, full stop on an old, unsustainable, kill-or-be-killed, "cold cruel world" competitive way of being. And she's asking us to instead connect, to remember who we are, to listen to our inner wisdom, and to live a different way. In essence, she's asking us to live connected, and to live in AWE.

And so, that's my final challenge to you. To look beyond what AWE can simply do for you, and, yes, as President Kennedy said (in my interpretation), ask what you can do with AWE to help others. For this truly is a time to move from the me to the we, from the egoic small self of what do I need, and what do I get to do, to how can I help others, how can I play a role, how can I serve? It's a time to recognize that we are all individual cells in the human beingness, one being, one humanity, and, for that matter, one planet as well. For what we do as individuals, such as tapping into AWE, affects the entirety of humanity and the entire planet.

This is a time to grow, to expand our consciousness, and to go from the small self, with a scarcity or lack-based mindset, to tapping into the incredible abundance of the Universe, to going from scared and alone, to a place of togetherness, oneness, and co-creation—that is how we will make it through this time and truly ascend to the upper room.

If we get it, that this is a time to plug in, to heal our wounds, to shine bright, and to lift others up, in essence, if we view this as a time to give back, serve, and come together as one, then we will be thanked by our kids, their kids, and perhaps even more than seven generations to come—as the Great Law of the Iroquois mandated, creating a sustainable world for all of humankind.

And we will raise the entirety of humanity, and a bit of consciousness itself, to a higher level. That is my hope, my dream, and hopefully the dream of all of humanity as well, at least in her brighter moments. For when we do this, it will change everything.

I challenge you: dive into AWE with everything you've got. For when you build a long-standing relationship with AWE, you can't help but cultivate your kindness, wisdom, and compassion for yourself and everyone around. Change your life, change the lives of those around you, and you could quite literally be changing the planet. For your highest good, and the highest good of all—or something better.

I send you love.

Resources

Websites: Join Michael Sandler online at the book's website: www
.AutomaticWriting.com. You'll find a wealth of additional information including access to his ongoing classes.

Navigate to www.AutomaticWriting.com/bonuses for bonus
materials such as theta brain-entrainment music downloads,
the ten-count meditation technique, and the 30-Day Challenge
worksheet.

Attend Michael Sandler's bootcamps, masterclasses and more
through www.InspireNationUniversity.com.

Discover your greatest morning routine to kick start your day,
and your life at www.MagicalRoutine.com.

Learn how to get your best night's sleep and set your days and
AWE up for success starting the evening before at www.Magical
EveningRoutine.com.

Tap into Michael Sandler's mindful running program at www
.MindfulRunning.org.

Podcast: Listen to Michael Sandler's top-rated self-help and spirituality *Inspire Nation* show at www.InspireNationShow.com.

YouTube channel: Watch Michael Sandler's inspirational show on YouTube and at www.YouTube.com/InspireNationShow

Books: Distinguished experts and their books mentioned in this book:
Rhonda Byrne, *The Secret*
Dawson Church, PhD, *Bliss Brain: The Neuroscience of Remodeling Your Brain for Creativity, Resilience and Joy*
Wayne Dyer, *Inspiration: Your Ultimate Calling*
Linda Geddes, *Chasing the Sun*
Kyle Gray (author of numerous books on angels)
Rick Hanson, *Hardwiring Happiness*
Mitch Horowitz, *The Miracle Habits*
Daniel Kahneman, *Thinking, Fast and Slow*
Howard Martin, *The HeartMath Solution (with Doc Lew Childre)*
Bradley Nelson, DC, *The Emotion Code*
Andrew Newberg, MD, *How Enlightenment Changes Your Brain* (with Mark Robert Waldman)
Dean Radin, PhD, *Real Magic*
Paul Selig, *I Am the Word; Beyond the Known: Realization; and Alchemy: A Channeled Text*
Robin Sharma, *The Monk Who Sold His Ferrari*

Articles: The link to Dr. Newberg's study of automatic writing practitioners is here: www.ncbi.nlm.nih.gov/pmc/articles/PMC3500298/.

Software: Free software called f.lux (www.justgetflux.com) can dim your computer screen at night so that you're not overstimulated by blue light.

Acknowledgments

First and foremost, to my Pookie, now upgraded to Pook-Star, Jessica Lee. You are my earth, you are my sun, you are my rock, you are my everything, and as our dear friend Hendrick Maako said, "Dude, you would be nowhere without her."

And to Jack Burden, my greatest mentor on either side of the veil, and my best man at eighty-nine years young. You were right, you were right, you were right. You could see my genius and where I was to go far before I ever could. Thank you beyond thanks. And yes, as you say, I'll keep taking better care of that Baby Doll!

To both Jessica and Jack, I dedicate this book—where would I be, without both of you?

I want to give a massive thanks to all of the teachers, wisdom keep-ers, wisdom seekers, clients, and guests on our show *Inspire Nation* who have come into my life. With special thanks to the many students and practitioners of automatic writing who have taken our course and volunteered to share their stories and even samples of their automatic writing for this book.

To everyone everywhere who has been a part of my journey, whether you've been a supporter, teacher, guide, or whether you've been on the other side, whatever that means. You are my teachers, you are my soul workers, you are my everything. Thank you.

To my family, to Jessica's family, and maybe, most of all, to all of the four-legged and two-legged critters and other creatures who have come into our lives, starting with Nacho Molé who has really been by my side in this journey. Thank you.

To our kitty cat Sir Meowsers, who has held space in each of our homes for all of this, to Lumi (aka Switch Blade) for his incredible love, to the Love Bug (aka Play Bug) for her incredible joy and love of life even as she's falling off a railing and down a twelve-foot flight of stairs. To Pumpkin, our coyote mix, who was with us through our first book tour. To my service dog, Sawa, who is still energetically by my side.

And to the latest edition of our family, Ruby Roo Roo the Wonder Rooster, thank you for pushing me outside of my comfort zone, my box, and my studio, and for helping me to see the world from an entirely new perspective—you are our clarion in life.

To Bam Bam, our cork-screw tailed Japanese Bobtail, for always being there by my side on Maui, you were and are pure love—we hope to see you again soon. To Koa Coon who crossed the ocean blue with us and whose time with us was far too short—boy did you know how to play!

To Aunty Puanani Mahoe (aka Aunty Pua), for guiding us on our journey on Maui and teaching us all about the aloha spirit. Thank you for your continued love, guidance and support from beyond. We send you love!

To Shen, one of our greatest teachers on Maui. You showed us how to tai chi energy, and use quantum love to hold a bigger brighter future for ourselves and those around us.

To Ceci Benavides, you are a true shaman and a true open-hearted warrior. You have taught us so much far beyond words. You have taught us the kind, gentle, easy, good, Papa Dear, Mama Dear way. Thank you for your love. Thank you for your guidance. And most of all, thank you for showing us that we don't need to be torn down in order to grow back strong.

To Marianne and Vinny Schoenfelder, can we give you angel couple of the decade? You helped us to fly free and got us from New Jersey to North Carolina to the Outer Banks, to your incredibly beautiful home and springboard to the West. You helped us both to grow our wings.

To Carla Solberg, your time with us, which was again far too short, means more than we could ever put in words. You are, were, and always will be a true angel to us. We love your laugh and I enjoy hearing it each and every time I write to you in AWE.

To Zach Bergen, another true spiritual brother from another mother. Thank you for your love, your support and your music. And thank you for quite literally marrying Jessica and me.

To Aya Murillo, you are our amazing spiritual sister in the Philippines. You have been there since the beginning. Thank you for helping us get our show off the ground and for all that you do!

To David Meredith, yet another spiritual brother and angel in time of need. Not only did you share with us your heart and aloha, but you helped us get off of Mother Maui. We love you David!

To Shaun Simmons, my soul brother, thank you so much for teaching us Ho'oponopono, for guiding us on such amazing journeys, for the most amazing music (*Learning to Fly* still makes me cry) and for teaching us, the mission IS love.

To Claudio, one of our most amazing meditation teachers on Maui. Thank you for being such an incredible tugboat into the deep, and setting such an amazing example.

To Denise Fisher, you are our angel. Why you came out to Lake Tahoe after my accident, when you had never met us and spent days there healing us, and then brought me back to your couch in your living room, moving around your entire life and house for me to heal enough to take a plane back to Maui, I cannot even begin to understand. Thank you so much for your kindness, your compassion, and all that you did for us.

To Jason Hobson, another spiritual brother, thank you for your support, your love and for helping us get on our feet when we needed it most. You have gone way above and beyond the duty as a friend and as a brother.

To Sian Chua, who helped introduce us to an automatic writing process through the Akashic Masters and for helping me see who I truly am, and where I'm meant to be, with your amazing Dolores Cannon past-life regression work.

To Richard Yiap, thank you so much for sharing THE light with us.

To Adam Brix, for encouraging, guiding and recording us on our early journey. How you managed to stay in the back of our little four-door mini hatchback crossover SX4 with the rear seats taken out, with two dogs in the car for one month on book tour, I have no idea. But thank you for being with us for all the "B-left" turns—and go Ha-le-a-kala!

To Dr. Ray McClanahan, another true spiritual brother, barefoot runner and healer. Thank you for all that you do in the world. Thank you for encouraging us, guiding us, and for your tremendous love and light—and helping to heal the world's feet.

To Laurie Huseby, for your generosity and your support. You are another tremendous angel in our lives.

To Richard Taubinger, for believing in us and helping us get out *Mindful Running*. It was your inspiration, vision, and *Mindful Running*

Summit, that got me started down the yellow brick road of interviews and on this *Inspire Nation* journey.

To Brenda Michaels, for helping us get the *Inspire Nation* show launched.

To CJ Liu, my weekly sister-in-arms . . . though there are no weapons involved. You've been there since the beginning of *Inspire Nation,* and BEFORE. You helped us launch, guided us, and are an amazing beacon of bright light. I send you all my love!!!

To Misha Crosby, thank you for your incredible editing assistance on our early shows, on our YouTube production, and all that you have done for us. You are not just an editor but a true friend.

To Sergiu Argesanu, another friend and brother at arms, and the most incredible editor when we needed you most—thank you for your joy, your love, and your infectious, jubilant enthusiasm. We can't wait to work with you again!

To Yannan Li, we love you. We cannot thank you enough for your assistance. You have helped us take our show and all that we do to an entirely new level.

To Carol Campos, another true unicorn and dream team member extraordinaire. Thank you so much for following your *Divine Breadcrumbs,* which have led your way here, and beyond!

To Marie-Rose Phan-Le, for your guidance, patience, and gentle, or not-so-gentle, prodding. You've helped us more than we have even begun to realize. Thank you so much.

To Scott Slack, for dropping everything and pausing your world to produce our Netflix pilot to help millions. How does it get any better than this—Hollywood here we come! Thank you so much for making such wondrous works of art out of our footage. I don't know how you did and do it!

To Lala, for your eye-catching graphic design, and to Dennis Deauna, for helping us birth our *Inspire Nation* rising phoenix logo and for taking our brand to the next level.

To Bhavik Patel, for your SEO, podcast and YouTube tinkering, and for allowing me to breathe easier at night.

To Dr. W. David Berglund, author of *Turning the Diet World Upside Down*, and Hua for working with us in proprioceptive kinesiology and helping us to scan and clean our "living computers".

To Anne Kimmer, our angel in the Roaring Forks Valley, for helping us to escape gravity—and saving our plants!

To Dean Arvidson and Marion Berner, our new high desert family for helping us get grounded, finish this book and see the stars!

To my sister Elisa Sandler Share, aka Elisa Lynee (www.ElisaLynee.com), you have been more of a creative inspiration than you ever could have imagined. Back in our earliest days when you were in drama, I was actually jealous. You actually encouraged me through your actions, not your words, to pick up drama myself, to get on stage, get behind the mic, and challenge me to come out of the creative closet and here I am today. I owe you a huge debt of gratitude. You had the courage to pick up for Broadway, New York, and even LA, and to make it in the music business, your way. You are a wayfarer on this path of creativity and of sharing your love, light, music, and healing voice with the world.

To my parents. Mom, Dad, I love you so much. Mom, I've got to be honest. I know you're probably still feeling guilty about my childhood, about how you believe you raised me. I want to let you know everything happens for a reason. Everything is perfect just as it is. You did the best you possibly could. You were and are THE most amazing mom. Both you and Dad have helped me to be the incredible person I am today. You did perfect. You did awesome. You did great. I love you guys so much.

To Dad, you are my rock star, a true angel in disguise, a mentor, a guide, a true open-hearted warrior, and you have taught me so much about how even despite fear, worries and concerns, how you can take it to a higher room and bring the most positive energy, vibration and laughter to this world. And you both found Mojo, how does it get any better than this!

To our childhood dog Sasha, and to the most amazing companion to my parents in the world, Gidget. Though you have passed on to the other side, your love goes on and on and on. Of course, I can't forget my childhood hamster Micaroo too. I wish I had done better, but you taught me so much about compassion. Thank you so, so much.

To my guardian angel Maximilian, thank you for keeping me safe, for protecting us and our beautiful home, and for always being by my side, since my earliest days, and perhaps far, far beyond that. Words cannot express how grateful I am to have you in our corner and by my side.

To G&D publishing, for believing in us and hanging in there. This year has been a wild ride and you helped us birth this beautiful book. We thank you so much, and believe the world will thank you too!

To Wayne Dyer, your books and words mean more to me than you could ever imagine. It was your book *Inspiration* that truly started me down this path. As you said in one of your earliest works, which launched me on my 5,000-mile, forty-day bike solo ride, "What could you do if you KNEW you couldn't fail?"

Near last, but certainly never least, to the archangels, Archangel Michael, Archangel Raphael, and Archangel Gabriel. Thank you for being there in AWE, in my coaching, in my classes, in my interviews, in my head, and in each moment of every action, and every day. Thank you for saving my life. And thank you for being my guiding lights to help me to help the world.

And to all angels, guides, and light workers, to my team on the other side of the veil, to Mother Earth, Mother Nature, to all the wee-beasties that make up my microbiome, this human space-ship I wear, and most of all to God, Source, Universe, or even, as I like to joke, the Giant Cheeseburger in the sky. If I could have a third dedication in this book, it would certainly be to you, the love that's all there is. You have guided me, kept me safe, kept me alive, and are my everything—far beyond this physical body.

You have truly tempered steel and softened me at the same time, helping me to become an open-hearted warrior, helping me to continuously learn, improve, to grow and to remain humble and connected to the earth. Thank you for your wisdom. Thank you for guidance. Thank you for helping me to help others. Thank you for all that you do to bring in the light, to help us be the light, to bathe us in love, and to help us to recognize the greatness of who we truly are. Thank you is not strong enough of an expression. So I can only say LOVE.

And if I didn't mention YOU, dear reader, I especially thank you, for being brave, for going on this journey, and sharing your love and light with the world! And hey, you made it to the end!

WOO HOO!!!

About the Author

MICHAEL SANDLER is the cohost of the popular *Inspire Nation* show, a transformational, self-help, spiritually focused podcast and YouTube channel, along with his wife, fellow coach, and teacher, Jessica Lee. He is a best-selling author, speaker, entrepreneur, visionary, coach, and the cocreator of *Inspire Nation* University and the *Automatic Writing Experience* online course.

Michael has taught automatic writing to thousands of people worldwide. Through his Open-Hearted Warrior training program, he has also helped thousands more transform their lives over the course of twenty-five years. He is on a mission to elevate consciousness and help the world to shine bright. Michael is known for his affinity for anything bright yellow and his high-energy "WOO HOO!"

Having been a world-class athlete and coach, competing at the international level in cycling, along with being a competitive speed-skater, Ironman triathlete, and runner, Michael has applied those same training skills to being a life coach to teachers, leaders, and visionaries. He is a life-long meditation practitioner and meditation teacher.

Racing at the professional level, competing in Europe, and even doing a 5,000-mile solo ride across the country, he understands that it takes commitment, training, and community to succeed in achieving lofty goals and big life dreams.

As coauthor of the international best-seller Barefoot Running, Michael was featured on the *BBC, CBS Early Morning Show, ABC's Healthy Living, National Public Radio, US Armed Forces Network, Martha Stewart Radio, Unity Church Radio,* and by *Health* magazine, *Men's Health, Shape, Women's Health*, and many more publications.

Two near-death accidents led to the conception of the *Inspire Nation* show, the creation of the Automatic Writing Experience, and the writing of this book. These devastating accidents led Michael to a much deeper understanding about the world, of Spirit, and of our connection to something greater than ourselves. He calls this "getting the big picture" and from that this book emerged.

On his *Inspire Nation* show, he has to date interviewed over 1,200 of the world's leading authors, experts, and spiritual masters. The lessons gleaned from these interviews have infused his life, coaching, and even his marriage, for he's had the opportunity to speak with many of the greatest minds on earth.

Michael and Jessica have produced over 2,000 shows on their thriving YouTube channel with over 50 million downloads on their worldwide podcast.

Once driven purely by performance and results as an endurance athlete, Michael survived the near-fatal accidents that cracked his heart open and helped him discover a kinder, gentler way of moving through life—one that arguably makes an even greater impact on others and the planet.

That's what he calls being an open-hearted warrior—and to his mission to elevate consciousness, shift humanity, and help people truly discover their greatest self.

Despite twin titanium femurs and hips, as a result of the accidents, he continues to run, skate, and play in the mountains or explore the world in an RV with Jessica and his three kitty cats, along with Roo Roo the Wonder Rooster—always in prayer, always connected to Spirit.

As Michael likes to say, "Spirit is my oxygen."

CPSIA information can be obtained
at www.ICGtesting.com
Printed in the USA
JSHW011009100523
41474JS00003B/5